RUNNING
MARK'S MARATHON –

The Making of a Mid-Life
Marathon Runner

Andrea-Louise Glenn

If you enjoy this book, please leave a review at the retailer you made your purchase from.

Also available as an ebook from most major retailers.

Credits for official race photography:

Virgin London Marathon 2013 – marathonfoto.com
Sibelco Dartmoor Vale Marathon 2013 – miraclepr.photium.com
Great Bristol 10k 2016 – marathon-photos.com

Interior layout by Jesse Gordon – adarnedgoodbook.com

Table of Contents

Introduction

Running Mark's Marathon -
The Making of a Mid-Life Marathon Runner

This book is the story, in journal style, of my journey from not terribly serious but glad to be getting fit again after ten years of child wrangling four times half-marathon finisher (try saying that without taking a breath), to first-time marathon runner and on beyond.

My hope is that in sharing my story, you may be inspired to believe that whatever age or stage of life you're at and whether you want to get one under your belt bucket-list style or hope it will be the first of many, you could run a marathon too.

I doubt that I would have found the courage or motivation to embark upon training for a marathon without the inspiration that came from the possibility of running the Virgin London Marathon 2013 in memory of my brother Mark and this book is dedicated to him.

Mark Richard Everingham
21st July 1973 - 29th June 2012

Journal Entry 1 – 23rd July 2012

A Mile for Mark

Today I ran an extra mile for Mark.

Mark is (or do I now say was?) the younger of my two step-brothers, who I grew up with from around the age of four. Mark took his own life just a few weeks ago.

Unbeknown to each other, having been out of touch for many years, Mark and I both took up running in 2010, myself at the age of 39 and Mark 37. Mark's long term partner Jelena recently told me that Mark had quickly become a very disciplined and dedicated runner and had been in training for the 2012 London marathon until injury forced him to stop running in the last few months before his death. Devastatingly for Mark, the recurrence of a long-term back problem and the resulting complications appeared to indicate that he could never hope to realise his potential as a runner. In fact it was possible that Mark felt, rightly or wrongly, that he would have to learn to live with constant pain and significant physical limitations and it seems likely that struggling to come to terms with all of this was one of the many factors that brought him to a place where life was too hard to keep on living.

So, I ran the mile for Mark because I now know that we shared a passion for running and I am both surprised and pleased by how much that knowledge means to me following his death. Since the first tentative strides of our respective running journeys, there would have been so much we could have spent hours talking about together (and boring the pants off the people around us with), so many experiences and aspirations we might have connected over, but, for reasons I can now never fully understand, over the last ten years Mark had ceased to respond to or initiate contact. The end of Mark's life has inevitably sealed the decision he appears to have made in this respect. It feels like it was a conscious decision to disconnect rather than just apathy, but to my knowledge not one made publicly, and it saddens me deeply that the friendship I felt we two had started to grow for the first time back in our twenties was not, as I'd believed then, the foundation for a genuine relationship as adults, but rather all there would ever be. I feel cheated. Running for Mark feels like a way that I can reconnect with him and, although he's gone now, that somehow feels really important to me. Maybe I can even take up the dreams that seemed lost to Mark.

My body protested at the exertion of running today, as it always seems to even though I know in reality I'm becoming stronger all the time, but I still managed a good pace especially considering it was one of the hottest days of the year so far. For most of the run I stayed at the head of a group of ten or so others from the women's running club I belong to. I have gradually developed the ability to run at a relatively respectable pace (that being relative to my age, experience and the amount of training I do or, more to the point, don't do) and often take up a position near the front of the group on our club nights. On a long run alone or running in a race, I really struggle to keep going for the full distance without the overwhelming desire, often indulged, to stop and walk for a bit and this is a source of frustration to me. I hope I can crack that in the future if I become a bit more intentional about the way I train; I probably need to take a leaf out of Mark's book.

So, the big question I have been asking myself over the last few weeks is this: do I have the ability and dedication to run a marathon in me, as Mark believed that he did? Could I even run a marathon in memory of Mark? Right now I don't know the answer to that, but for today, instead of settling for a safe four mile run as I generally have done recently, I decided to run an extra mile for Mark.

The Academic and the Stay-at-Home Mum

Before we progress further along this journaling journey together, I should offer a little background about Mark and myself. It will be brief but hopefully insightful.

At the age of ten, Mark won a full scholarship to a prestigious private school in Bristol, Clifton College. Back then it was a boys school. Mark wasn't a typical Clifton College boy, at that time having a strong aversion to school sports in any form and determinedly avoiding games lessons whenever he could, but he did very well academically, so much so that when his GCSE results came through the school rapidly reversed their previous decision that he should continue his studies at another educational establishment because of his refusal to fit in with their ethos; he was suddenly worth keeping hold of. In a two-fingered salute to their establishment, Mark instead chose to study for his A levels at one of the local further education colleges, going on to pursue a successful career through Manchester, Bristol, Oxford and Leeds Universities as a world leader in the field of research into computer vision.

As the tributes on Mark's web page read, he was not only extremely clever (many have said a genius) but also scientifically rigorous, inspirational, caring, funny, generous and humble. And he wasn't just a computer geek, his knowledge and experience definitely not being confined to his chosen career niche. My sister-in-law Louise's comment after Mark's funeral was, "He sounded like a great guy!" echoing the sentiments of those who wish we'd known him better in life. I very much doubt that Mark was able to see in himself all the special qualities other people did. It's true that there were a good handful of difficult characteristics about Mark that caused distress to people in his world and possibly he was over aware of these in himself, but we're none of us perfect and, for someone who had a rough start in life, neither are they perhaps surprising.

Mark had applied the same commitment and passion he'd brought to his field of research to his running; he was not one to do things by halves, tending towards perfectionism. His ability as a runner had been developed through study (attending courses and reading books), self-discipline (in his training and healthy lifestyle) and determined goal setting. I can imagine that he saw in running a way of not only improving his health as he'd suffered from back problems for several years, but also his whole quality of life, perhaps even a way of achieving mastery and triumphing over his internal struggles. In March 2012 in training he'd run the half-marathon distance of 13.1 miles in 1:44 and, I imagine, was hoping to run London marathon in well under four hours. Not too bad for someone who for most of his childhood had probably believed he wasn't sporty.

And myself? I got along ok, both academically and socially, at the local state school that called itself a Grammar School, although I was never sure what that distinction actually meant in practice. I left with the expected nine O levels and three A levels, expected by the school and by my parents, with a spread of grades that reflected both my ability (it was there) and my enjoyment of academic study (I didn't). The maxim 'could try harder' would have accurately described my academic years but I can't remember if it actually ever did make an appearance on any of my school reports. From my point of view, yes, I could have tried harder, but I just wasn't ever inspired to do so. I was ok at school sports and would have a go at most, but in terms of being physically active ballet was my true passion from an early age. Further education and paid work saw me travel through an interesting mix of dance, medical laboratory science and social work before landing where I am now as a married mum of four and home educator.

I wouldn't know where to start in listing my personal characteristics, but hopefully some of those will show through in my writing so I can avoid the task of trying to describe myself to you. For now I'll just say that I can't claim excellence in any area of life, I'm a fairly ordinary girl really. I had some Christian input in my earlier teenage years after my mum became a born-again Christian and came to that decision myself too at the age of 28, so my faith is a big part of my identity and my outlook on life. I confess to often having little idea of what's going on in the world at large with being so absorbed in the small world of my own family. I wish I could make more time to relax with my kids and keep house well (they seem mutually exclusive goals most of the time). I'm generally just an average kind of person with nothing particular to distinguish me, but I hope that the things I apply myself to in life I do to the best of my ability.

As a runner, I always want to improve, to run faster or longer, but I'm not very good at consistently finding the discipline that requires. Not to be too hard on myself, I suppose having my children around all the time (and as we home educate, I really do mean all the time) also makes that tricky. I wouldn't say that I love the act of running in itself or that I find it therapeutic as some do, rather that I enjoy feeling and looking fit again after ten years of child rearing without an exercise regime and I'm still amazed that after years of relative neglect my body will respond to regular running and I can achieve things I had never imagined possible even in my youth. My prayer as I run is often one of thanks to God, for in experiencing how my body responds to physical training I am experiencing the truth that we are, to quote Psalm 139, 'fearfully and wonderfully made'. Up to now I've run one 10k race and four half-marathons steadily improving on my times and I'm sure there's more running potential to be tapped in me if I can carve out the time and find the determination. I hope it will be tapped.

So Mark and I came to running for different reasons and invested in it our hope for different kinds of satisfaction, but essentially we had both been gripped at the same point in time by this fantastically simple sport that, with the acquisition of suitable footwear (plus the essential sports bra for us ladies) and a reasonable level of health, is truly open to all.

Journal Entry 3 – 30th July 2012

A Scheme Begins to Take Shape

I ran with the running club I belong to, Sole Sisters, again tonight, reverting back to my safe four mile run as we'd had a busy week full of summer holiday activities and enjoying friends' paddling pools in the sunshine, in the course of which I hadn't managed to make time for any more runs since last week's club night. Actually, I confess, I probably could have found the time if I was able to get over the mental hurdle of leaving the house to run on my own; I find it so much easier to run with company. So I opted for the four mile route over the other possibilities of five or six miles, in anticipation of heavy under-exercised unco-operative muscles, but, in that inexplicable manner that I imagine other runners may be familiar with, in fact I had a fantastic run and could comfortably have gone on for longer. There were some good conversations as we ran too which gave wings to the idea that has been taking shape for me since being in Leeds for Mark's funeral on the 20th July. But I'll come back to that newly airborne idea in a minute.

I returned from Leeds with a selection of books about running from Mark's fairly substantial collection; a good sized, slightly dusty stack of books that lived beside his bed. I have a similar stack of books beside my bed but not so many of them about running until now. Jelena, realising that I shared Mark's passion for running, had generously allowed me to take whatever books I liked after she had shown me around the house they lived in together, pointing out his collection of guitars (I had no recollection that he'd played, or maybe I never knew) and fitness equipment.

Back in Bristol, the first book I chose to read was Haruki Murakami's autobiographical 'What I Talk About When I Talk About Running'. Murakami makes this comment about his strength as a runner.

'I've never been injured, never been hurt and haven't been sick once. I'm not a great runner, but I'm definitely a strong runner'.

I think I'm a strong runner too overall, but I have been injured, I have been hurt (I'm not sure where the distinction lies between those two) and I do sometimes get sick (although interestingly I think much less so since I started running, often the coughs, colds and flus now seem to pass me by). I'm currently making a slow return to full running fitness after an injury that I developed while training for and running my last half-marathon in March, that being my second year running Bath half-marathon. I ran a time of 2:12, my fastest half-marathon to date and ten minutes faster than the previous year, but I was really hoping to run it in 2:10 or less which would have put my pace at just under ten minutes per mile and those extra minutes felt a real disappointment as I limped around over the following weeks with a groin injury that would then take ten weeks to fully heal. Feeling so strongly about a couple of minutes sounds ridiculous now I see it in writing, but I'm guessing I'm not alone in the celebration of a faster time being overshadowed by frustration that a personal goal wasn't met. When I ran my first half-marathon, my achievement in completing the race in a reasonable time for a woman of my age and circumstances (I was 39, had trained from zero active fitness in four months the best I could around family life and summer holidays and completed the course in 2:32) was swallowed up in my annoyance that I hadn't managed to run the whole distance non-stop and had committed the hideous crime of walking a bit (cue gasps of horror from the 'serious' runners). I have yet to experience elation, or anything remotely close in fact, on crossing a finish line, but I was solidly satisfied with my second and third half-marathon times (2:22 and 2:15), because I could see that I was steadily improving. Maybe I'm just not the type to experience elation on crossing the finish line, I'm normally just glad not to have to run a single step further.

Fortunately I haven't had any running injuries that have had long-term effects and, so far, I've been able to avoid the expensive treatments I have heard others talk about from physiotherapists and sports masseurs. I am of course at an advantage in being married to Pete, a highly skilled practitioner of the Chinese healing arts, who I have to call upon regularly to manipulate my back back to the line it should be in, normally when I've put it out after hunching over a computer keyboard for hours. Hmmm, I am writing this whilst hunching over a computer keyboard, I really should learn my lesson. Pete is also able to administer post-race treatments for those aching muscles. While I'm celebrating the benefits of free treatment, I shouldn't fail to make mention of those wonderful people that have offered massage in the runner's village after I've run for the cancer charity Clic Sargent, their pummeling of my fatigued muscles has been right up there with the pleasure of eating the Mars Bar from my post-race goodie bag (sort of free if you don't count the fee paid to enter the race) and a hot bath after (mostly) running 13.1 miles.

So, to return to my growing idea and tie the first two paragraphs together, the second book from Mark's collection that I'm currently a few chapters into reading is 'The Non-Runner's Marathon Trainer' by Whitsett, Dolgener & Kole. The authors maintain that anyone, health issues notwithstanding, can complete a full marathon if they follow their training schedule. I'm convinced already, about three chapters in, that this is a reasonable claim and, by that token, I could run a marathon myself. So here's my now helium-filled, bobbing on the end of a piece of string scheme: What if I could take Mark's actual place for the London marathon and run it in his memory? I feel excited and nervous in equal measure as I ponder this possibility, but also aware that I need to consider, before I take things any further, whether this is a worthwhile ambition to pursue given the time and energy that I will need to invest in training for a marathon. Is this something that merits such an investment of myself when I'm already wall-to-wall busy with family life? Could it bear fruit for us all as a project beyond simply my own satisfaction, or might it be something the pursuit of which comes at the expense of family and other priorities? I think my first steps will be to run the idea by Jelena and, if she's in agreement with the idea in principle, to contact the event organisers and see if Mark's place had been deferred to 2013 and, if so, can possibly be transferred to me. If this marathon ball looks like it's going to roll, and at the moment it feels like a big ball to get rolling, then hopefully I will see a green light in that (perhaps too many metaphors going on here) and feel able to commit and say, yes, I'm really going to do this. My personal faith in a God who is intimately concerned with and involved in the detail of my life means that prayer will be part of my process too. Watch this space to find out if I let go of the string and allow my marathon balloon to fly.

Journal Entry 4 – 6th August 2012

Loving the Hills, Taking the Plunge and a Reflection

I ran a very satisfactory five and a bit miles with Sole Sisters tonight (and believe me those bits are significant), taking on some of Bristol's famous hills. The choice of distance had been agreed upon with resolve by myself, close friend Clare and newly-made-that-evening friend Carrie at the previous week's club night as we basked in the sweaty afterglow of a good run. Running and chatting through the miles alongside someone is a great way to get to know them, assuming of course that you both have enough breath to talk and don't just want to stay in your own headspace doing battle with your running demons.

A Sole Sisters club night goes something like this: members descend on that week's meeting venue (an assortment of venues are used around the north of the city) and from the choice on offer for that evening, which depends on how many group leaders are available, individuals select their desired distance and their pace, from steady or faster. We get a brief description of the route and then we set off, regrouping at various points along the way. There are normally loud groans if the route includes hills and I would have been amongst the groaners in my first year to eighteen months of running, but my body has adapted gradually and now I actually love the hills. My breathing becomes more laboured with the extra exertion of running uphill, my lungs and legs feel the burn, but I can keep going to the top now, gone are the days when my legs turned to lead halfway up and I would have to stop and walk the rest. It is so satisfying to feel progress in my running and my overall level of fitness in spite of my intermittent pattern of exercise.

At this point, as you read my musings, I feel that I should acknowledge that you may be wondering how I could have the audacity to imagine that I could run a full marathon when, based on my diary so far, I only appear to run once a week. Point taken. In response I will offer the reassurance that I have actually run more often in preparation for previous races; I've aimed for three times a week but often only managed twice in reality, with the odd swim session thrown in too. I have increased my distances to long runs of around ten miles in preparation for half-marathons. The bigger issue that I'm identifying as I read through the, really very good, Non-Runner's Marathon Trainer, is the lack of method in my previous training as I have not followed a programme developed by people with experience. There perhaps lies the source of my recent injury, I wonder if I upped my mileage too quickly on 'The Andrea Plan - tried and tested by no-one with any sense' without putting in the quantity of weekly runs required or making a gradual incremental increase in distance so that my body could adapt properly to the requirements I was placing on it. Hey, listen to me, I almost sound like I know what I'm talking about, but only because I just read that advice in The Non-Runner's Marathon Trainer.

Feeling a boost of confidence after tonight's run, I took the plunge and sent a text to Jelena to sound her out on the idea of running the London marathon in Mark's place in his memory and, yes, I'll admit I did hesitate over the send command for a minute knowing that just the act of sharing the idea starts making it real. Jelena replied that she was happy with the idea and would send me any paperwork she could find referring to his place so I can find out firstly if he had deferred the place to 2013 and secondly, if he had indeed deferred, whether I could run in his place. So, the first small step has been taken. Gulp. The further I read through the aforementioned Non-Runner's Marathon Trainer, the more certain I feel that a marathon is fully achievable with the right attention to training. In fact I might even be a little disappointed if I can't have a go now.

Reflecting on why this journal started, It is over a month now since Mark took his life and somewhat disappointingly I find that the hard, cold reality of that act and of his death has already disappeared from my day-to-day consciousness. I say disappointingly because I'm saddened that I can apparently process and move on from such a significant event so quickly. Perhaps that's not surprising given that we hadn't been part of each others lives for such a long time and that our worlds had been entirely separate, but also I think that the way Mark chose to die and all the details he'd given attention to around that decision made the statement that death was absolutely what he wanted, it was in no way a cry for help that went too far. It's strange that with such intentionality the impact of the act of suicide feels diminished to me so that it almost becomes purely a matter of individual choice in the manner of leaving a job or ending a relationship one was unhappy in, something that's only newsworthy until the next story breaks.

Whilst it may seem all too easy for me accept and move on from Mark's death, I know that will not be true for Jelena, his partner of sixteen years. Hers will be a very different grief with pain, questions and doubt being dragged in its wake. I am thankful to Jelena for loving Mark in the way she did, particularly in the absence of good relationships with his family, and recognise that she is the one who will bear the deepest pain and whose life has been the most immediately and profoundly impacted by his death. I ponder on the hopeless place Mark must have been in to choose death and I'm so sad that ultimately he saw no other way out.

From recent conversations with Jelena and from seeing the physical evidence of Mark's passion for running in all his acquired paraphernalia, it seems that Mark had invested a great deal of himself over the last few years in running and, I read between the lines, not solely as a means of improving his health and fitness but also the whole quality of his life. It must have been crushing to have that hope removed as Mark struggled with the extent of his back problems, the resulting complications and his prognosis, as he perceived it. As someone who has also existed for many years in a state of mental and emotional fragility and then found hope and healing (myself in relationship with God), I can relate to the profound effect there would be in having that hope snatched away and being returned to the former inferior plane of existence. Perhaps I'm investing too much meaning in those events, but they help me to feel for Mark and to identify with a small part of his psyche. I wish I had known that living was so difficult for him. I wish it had been in my power to do something to make a difference. You were important to me Mark and I don't want to forget you so easily. I like to imagine that I connect with the deep significance that running held for you and training for and running your marathon would be a way for me to declare to you beyond the grave that I did care deeply.

Journal Entry 5 – 27 August 2012

A Running Intermission

Hmm, a slight spanner in the works, I have broken a bone in my foot and been told that I shouldn't run on it for at least six weeks - gah! That does still allow me enough time to train to run the marathon in spring if I can get the place, but I'll return to that storyline in a paragraph or two.

I ran again with Sole Sisters a week after my last entry, a run of just over five miles. That week the final half a mile, tipping us over a precise five, was intentional as the five and six-mile groups had merged for the evening. It was another good run for me, but a tough one with more hills. Knowing that I'd miss the following week's club night as I'd be away camping with Clare and the children, I'd been considering how I might make up for it the week after whilst at my mother-in-law's in Lincolnshire with the family. I calculated that I could capitalise on the abundance of childcare and extra time to get myself out running most days, even if just for my familiar round-the-block three and a bit mile circuit. I thought perhaps my holiday running plan could help kick start a more regular running programme once back at home, but of course I hadn't bargained on myself and my four year old son George picking up a collection of injuries while setting up camp in Charmouth, Dorset. Within minutes of each other,

George had broken his collarbone in a stunt man style head-over-heels tumble down the grassy bank in front of our tent and I (somewhat less glamorously) had fractured the top of a bone in my second toe by unwittingly leaving it behind me tangled in a bag strap while the rest of me moved away with purpose - YEOUCH!

Despite our accidents, we weren't in a too much discomfort so long as no-one poked, pushed or trod on us in the wrong place, so after a trip to the nearest Accident and Emergency Department twenty miles away we were able to continue with our three nights of camping and had a great time in a two day window of glorious sunshine. On arriving back in Bristol, George and I, as instructed, headed straight off to our local hospital, explanatory letters and x-ray disks in hand, to sort out our follow-up treatment. Two extremely tedious hours of waiting later, imagine my shock and dismay to be politely informed by an obviously flustered and embarrassed doctor, that I had failed to wait for treatment at the hospital in Dorset and a referral would therefore need to be made to Social Services as this was a Child Protection issue. This did explain why the doctor in Dorset's "All the best then!" farewell to us had felt like he was communicating that he was finished with us whilst simultaneously leaving me wondering why George hadn't been supplied with a sling or myself any support for my foot; we had obviously been expected to wait for someone else to attend to us. It does help if things are explained clearly to those of us who aren't Accident and Emergency veterans. I had scratched my head, and various other people's, on leaving the hospital in Dorset as to why we had apparently been dismissed without our full treatment (maybe, I reasoned, it was a cost-cutting exercise so that pesky holiday-makers wait for proper treatment until they're back in their own health trust area) and I had plundered the first-aid kit in the car and made George a sling myself. Meanwhile there must have been a nurse scratching his or her head and wondering where we'd disappeared to. Good communication was missing on both sides it would seem.

Well, after a call to the local Social Services children and families team the next morning, who had indeed received a referral, and a phone conversation with a social worker, it seems that the miscommunication and misunderstanding has been communicated and understood. Here's hoping that's the end of it, but if it doesn't turn out to be, you will get the next installment at a later date. Being officially a cause for concern plays havoc with a good night's sleep; after being thus informed, that night I dreamt about social workers going through the minutiae of our lives down to the crayons the children use, whilst Pete dreamt he was fending them off outside the house with a samurai sword! I do understand why protocol must be followed for those instances where there may be real child welfare issues that might otherwise be missed, but it feels truly horrible to be the object of suspicion when you know that's not the case.

So, dramas aside, time to fill in where I've got to with the marathon idea. Jelena sent to me an official letter from the organisers of the London marathon, Mark's offer of a place to run the marathon in 2012. The letter stated that the place could be deferred for a year in the event of there being a legitimate reason why the participant can't run. Jelena was unsure whether Mark had deferred when his health problems meant he had to stop running in March 2012 and, to add to the uncertainty, I have now unhelpfully managed to lose the letter which had his individual reference number on it. Neither of these unknowns are insurmountable issues in themselves, but in a moment of doubt whilst looking at the official website a few nights ago to find the organisers contact details, I came across a section about charity entries and decided to experimentally fill out a form for a charity place for 2013, running to raise funds for Samaritans. If I were to run with a charity place, I would probably need to commit to raising between £1000-£2000, but I think that would be achievable. I imagine that if I up the stakes for myself by running 26.2

miles, doubling anything I've attempted before, my good friends and family (and hopefully some of Mark's friends too) would match that with their financial generosity.

As well as investigating the charity avenue incase I'm not be able to take Mark's marathon place, I've also been wondering if running in Mark's actual place in some ways presumes that he would have thought that fitting. Maybe he wouldn't have, maybe he'd be thinking, "Get your dirty running shoes off my marathon place. If I couldn't run it, why should you get to?". Perhaps getting a place to run in my own right acknowledges that this is more about me; me finding a way to keep Mark's memory alive for a while longer for myself and finding a way to reconnect with him by putting myself through the miles and mustering the mental discipline that he had done on his own marathon journey. I will see if I get a positive reply from Samaritans and decide where to take it from there.

Four and a half weeks until I can start running again.

An Update on My Thought Process

I'm back in Bristol after our annual summer visit to Lincolnshire and having trawled through a 2 week backlog of emails - yes, I'm a dinosaur; I don't yet have my email set up so I can get it on my mobile when I'm away from home - I see that I don't have a response from Samaritans about my request to run London marathon and fundraise for them. (Aargh, I'm itching to say 'The' Samaritans because it sounds better, but on the website there is no The in front.) It could just be that no one has dealt with my application yet, but in the absence of an answer my starting point of trying to run in Mark's own marathon place has come back into focus. I am also putting aside my ramblings about whether Mark would have appreciated the gesture in order to consider a new angle. Mark's Dad, John, has recently received a letter from the charity Place2Be expressing their sincere gratitude for donations made by Mark's friends since his death. In his will, it transpires, Mark had chosen this charity - who do work in schools supporting children to deal with personal issues that can lead to emotional, behavioural and hence educational problems - for people to donate to instead of buying flowers for his funeral.

His estate would also have gone to them had there been some reason it could not go to Jelena. Knowing this now, it feels like it would be exciting if I could raise more funds for them through sponsorship, but the catch is that they are not a charity who are regularly allocated places for the London marathon. So, if you are able to connect my thought process dots, taking Mark's marathon place begins to look like the best option again in that it gives me the opportunity to fundraise for a cause obviously close to Mark's heart. So Mark, my apologies if you may not have appreciated the sentiment in me running your race, but I hope you would have been pleased to know that your chosen charity could benefit further through my sweat, blisters and all the rest. So, tomorrow I need to get on the blower to the London marathon organisers; I really must stop beating around the bush now.

Mark's academic memorial event (that sounds clumsy, but I'm not sure yet what the official title is) is on the 17th in Leeds and I am trying to get my head round the logistics of childcare so that I can be there. As I understand it, it will be a little like an afternoon conference with speakers from his area of expertise, computer vision, celebrating Mark and his contribution to the field, followed by food and drink. I'm sure most of the academic content will be well over my head, but I think the organisers are keen for family to be there and I find that hearing about the bits of Mark's life that I didn't know or experience firsthand helps to compensate a little for those missing ten years.

My foot is healing well; the bruising is almost gone, the toe is just a little swollen still and hurts a lot if bumped. My home-made treatment - on Pete's recommendation - is a daily ginger foot-bath; powdered ginger is heated though in boiling water and my foot is immersed in the mixture for a soak with the water being as hot as I can take it without scalding myself. The result is a satisfying warm tingly afterglow in the area of the injury, the effect of the ginger being, and here I will turn to consult Pete who is sat beside me, to tonify the muscle, bring extra blood into the area and help to drive calcium into the bone, I quote.

Journal Entry 7 – 4th September 2012

It's Actually Going to Happen!

I bit the bullet, I finally stopped blustering and did it, I made the call. Mark had deferred his London marathon place to 2013 and I can take it on! There were no hoops to jump through, nobody needed talking round to the idea, no arms needed twisting or heart strings pulling, I simply got a totally straightforward "Yes". All I have to do is email my details so that the place can be transferred into my name. Wow, I wasn't expecting it to be that easy, hence putting if off for so long; it really is going to happen!

Pete was there when I made the call, but, being a seriously big newsflash, a flurry of texts to other significant people was also called for: Clare, Jelena and my mum for starters. Excellent, Clare and Jelena have already said they'll come and support me on the day. Clare sent back a reply asking me how I felt about the idea actually becoming a reality and I replied, "Excited!" When I've thought about running a full marathon in the past, the idea has both intrigued and a terrified me in unequal measures (guess which had the edge?), but oddly now I don't feel scared at all. I'm not sure if I have the calm assurance of The Non-Runner's Marathon Trainer to thank for this confidence or whether it's the peace that comes when a door opens and you know that whatever lies on the other side of that threshold that the right thing to do is go ahead and cross it.

I have a few months before I will need to commence my training in earnest; enough time for my broken bone to knit well, to plan my running programme and to read and digest all the pearls of wisdom from The Non-Runner's Marathon Trainer (I really love that book). On my shopping list is an academic year diary so I can start scheduling my training runs. No winging it this time, I have to get serious now.

Journal Entry 8 – 5th October 2012

Up and Running Again

I waited the full six weeks (but not a day more) and six days ago I went out on my own for my first run since breaking my toe. I ran 3.43 miles - I had my running GPS watch on, hence the precision - and my toe is fine. My muscles and lungs however were not so fine; I am somewhat out of shape and my legs were very wobbly when I stopped. I determined to try and keep running through the discomfort of being unfit and just slow down as I needed to, so I only paused briefly to cross roads. One of my weaknesses as a runner (I think) is walking when it starts to feel like hard-going instead of pushing on through, but I'm thinking that one doesn't want to do too much walking when there's over twenty six miles to cover running a marathon, so I need to train myself in the discipline of mental, as well as physical, endurance. I need to deal with that voice in my head that shouts "This is too hard, I want to stop!" and train it to say something more along the lines of "Yes, this hurts, but I CAN keep going, I can do this". It will be beneficial to be practicing that all the way through my marathon training I think, even in the humble, out-of-shape beginning stages, so on my first post-injury run I made that determined decision.

I was pretty achy after that run, but I ran again four days

later, this time 2.65 miles (a tenth of a marathon) without stops. It was equally hard. I'm managing just under ten minute miles, which I'm happy with given my time off. Even when I'm in better shape I don't, yet, tend to run faster than nine and a bit minute miles. I felt a bit under the weather before I went for the second run this week, but decided to go anyway and I've been fine since, so perhaps I ran whatever it was out of my system.

My aim is to run short distances two to three times a week through October and November, then in December I'll step up to the four times a week that I'll need to commit to to be ready for the marathon and also begin to increase the mileage. I can't get back to Sole Sisters for a few weeks due to singing-related commitments, so I shall be doing most of my runs alone for the time being. The church I am part of are busy preparing for a big weekend of events to celebrate the completion of a project to convert a big warehouse style building in a local business park into our place of worship, so there is much painting, sawing, singing and all manner of other industrious activity filling people's every spare moment. I shall need to master the art of plugging into my iPod and learning an alto harmony whilst running over the next few weeks I think.

I had a slight panic a few days ago after reading an email from my running club saying that most members who had applied had now received notification in the post from the organisers of the London marathon to say whether or not they had a place for 2013, because I have had no official confirmation of my place. I decided rather than worrying to email the organisers and sure enough it turns out that they had not processed the transfer but have now said they will do so and I should receive a race pack in the post next week. Phew, I'm glad I contacted them.

It's good to be up and running again and to feel like my marathon training is actually underway. London, here I come!

Journal Entry 9 – 19th October 2012

A Lot of Singing
and a Little Running

I am gradually getting back into shape. I ran 3.5 miles straight through a few days ago and felt like I had a little more energy left in the tank at the end of the run. The week before I ran twice, including a run from the workshop where I'd left my car (hoping on the fourth attempt the automatic gearbox might finally get fixed) on to my hairdressers. Logistically that involved my mum meeting me at the garage so I could transfer the children into her care for the afternoon. I have to be innovative about fitting in running when life is busy and that worked out pretty well, apart from the distance, at a meagre 1.65 miles from garage to hairdresser, being shorter than I'd guessed it would be. My lovely hairdresser, Chrissy, who I've been going to for nearly twenty years (she's that good) didn't mind me turning up on her doorstep all sweaty and gave me lots of complements on how well I was looking since I'd started running, as well as the usual excellent haircut.

This week seems to have flown by though, without me fitting in a second run. In theory I could run early tomorrow before getting all the children ready to go out to the church launch service and party (the end goal of all the singing rehearsals and, yes, I did listen to my alto harmonies while on my last run), but I'm not a morning person and I don't enjoy forcing myself to get up and go straight out for a run, in fact I have deliberately avoided any early morning runs over the last few weeks on principle. Alternatively I could go out tonight after my eldest daughter's swimming lesson, which would mean running in the dark. Or, I could just admit defeat until after the weekend given that it's going to be such a busy one. Hmm, decisions. I would probably agonise over when to run less if I enjoyed the act more, but at the moment it's a bit like forcing yourself to take the nasty medicine because you believe it's good for you. I have a bit of an enthusiasm deficit.

I've started reading another of Mark's running books, 'Run Less, Run Faster' by Pierce, Muir & Ross, a training programme where you (only!) run three times a week and cross-train twice, apparently with great results as the title would suggest. I think it looks a bit too fiddly for me right now. There are different types of runs (track repeats, tempo and long runs), rather than just racking up the mileage week by week, and the marathon training programme assumes that you can run twenty miles by the third or fourth week and I'm way off that kind of fitness yet. The tone of the following quote nicely illustrates why this programme isn't for me.

> *The popularity of the marathon has resulted in the participation of runners with a vast divergence of talent. Marathon times have increased to an average of over four hours, with many runners still on the road five to six hours after the start.*

Hmm, my measure of 'talent', an interesting choice of word, will probably see me finishing the marathon in around five hours. I sense a little disapproval in the 'over four hours' comment let alone the 'still on the road five to six hours after the start' bit, so I think I'll leave the Run Less, Run Faster programme to the talented runners and stick with the Non-Runner's Marathon Trainer for myself, where the more encouraging authors suggest that the first-time marathoner should definitely not aim for a specific finish time rather just aim to get to the finish and celebrate that achievement.

Sadly I've nearly read all the running books that I took from Mark's collection, so if I want to read any more in that category I shall have to start buying them myself or finding them in the library. I do have my eye on a few that were prominently displayed in Waterstones recently, I imagine to appeal to the Olympics inspired would-be athletes amongst us. In the last few weeks, besides poking my nose briefly into Run Less, Run Faster, I have also read Mark's copy of 'Just a Little Run Around the World' by Rosie Swale Pope. Once I'd got far enough into Rosie's amazingly matter of fact account of her run around the world - yes, really, around the world - for my head to understand that she is not an ordinary woman so she doesn't give the kind of details an ordinary woman like me might wonder about, I found the book really enjoyable. Initially I struggled with her lack of explanation for how she was able to run all day when some of us are ready to give up and turn around by the time we reach the end of the road. But, that rather large information gap aside, what an amazing woman. It's not just the distance that she covered that is incredible (it took five years and fifty three pairs of shoes), but also the extreme conditions that she endured running through Siberia and Alaska camping out alone nearly all the way and carrying or towing all her own equipment. I repeat: what an amazing woman. It is astounding the feats of endurance that humans can come through intact. This marathon will certainly be mine.

Journal Entry 10 – 30th October 2012

Too Gung-Ho?

To refer back to the previous chapter, the outcome was that I admitted defeat, so that was a week with only one run. However, I made up for it last week by fitting in three - my first back with Sole Sisters running club since breaking my toe (4.5 miles) and two on my own (3.2 and 2.9 miles). I ran with Sole Sisters again last night (5.3 miles) but all the way through I had some discomfort that felt like shin splints and some niggly feelings in my left knee and hip. I felt much more conscious than usual of the impact of each step and I was really stiff and uncomfortable when I got out of bed this morning. Boo. I feel frustrated and concerned to be experiencing niggles so early on in my training, so I plan to wait three or four days and let things settle down and not go out running tomorrow as I'd intended. When I do run again I'll take it really steady and see how I feel. Dipping into a few running books to look up causes of shin splints and to try and identify why I might be struggling, it seems that pushing myself harder before I'm physically ready and therefore placing too much stress on my untrained body could be the reason. Other possibilities are running in worn-out trainers (I don't think I've run far enough in my current pair of reasonable quality running shoes for that to be the case), doing lots of hill running (not guilty there either) and having a poor running style. I imagine that there's always room for working on one's running style, but, in so far as self-assessment can be a realistic measure, I'm happy that mine is ok. Shortly after I started running Pete gave me a book called 'ChiRunning' by Danny & Katherine Dreyer (which I highly recommend) and as a result of reading it I made some mechanical adjustments to the way I run.

To throw some light on what ChiRunning is, let's see how well I can recall some of the basic premises for you. I've realised that it might be time I re-read the book after yesterday's running experience, so maybe I can fill in the gaps in my explanation once I have. Hmmm.... where to start? Ok, so the overall concept is that the majority of runners (and right now I am a prime example, despite having read the book and practiced some of the techniques) will experience injury as a result of stresses caused by running style and practice that is not working in harmony with either the body or the environment we run in and consequently becomes overly dependent on forced effort and the strength of the peripheral muscles alone. In contrast, the ChiRunning technique emphasises the importance of natural movement (understanding and utilising the body's built-in running ability), harnessing the effects of gravity to make it work in your favour, and core strength and stability. Chi energy is also talked about but I'm not knowledgeable enough to attempt to explain that.

Harnessing the effects of gravity in your running simply means making use of the falling-forward momentum that occurs when your centre of gravity is shifted as you stand upright then lean your body from the ankles. Try it for yourself now. As you lean forward from the ankles you'll sense gravity taking over and you'll have to throw a leg out in front to stop yourself falling. The runner, rather than needing to use muscle power and force to generate forward propulsion, thinks of tipping the whole body forward from the ankles in a straight line and can then translate that falling-forward pull of gravity into natural, freely available running power. The activation of the legs is what turns that downward if-something-doesn't-happen-here-my-face-is-going-to-splat-into-the-pavement pull of gravity into forward motion. Clever. Other aspects of ChiRunning that I have incorporated include a mid-foot strike (rather than heel or toe striking) and having a relaxed leg swing so that the leg unfolds loosely forward with each stride rather than being forcefully thrust out ahead. I am very overdue for refreshing myself in all the ChiRunning principles and re-applying them (Danny Dreyer recommends re-reading the book once a year) and doing so may help with my effort-induced aches and pains. Possibly too much forced effort and poor form has crept into my running over and above natural movement, which is why my body is currently struggling to cope with the extra demands I'm placing on it.

I now own two copies of the ChiRunning book as Mark had one too. I just had to take his copy, along with the other running books I chose from his collection, when I saw how well used it had been (with lots of different coloured sticky notes identifying pages he obviously wanted to refer back to) and knowing how important the book has also been to me. Apparently Mark attended a ChiRunning course when he first took up running. I think it's amazing that it has been so significant to both of us as we started out on our completely separate running journeys, particularly as I've yet to meet another runner who has used, or even heard of, the technique.

I now have an update to follow on from journal entry 5. I had a phone call a few weeks ago from one of the local council's education officers, I think as a result of the Social Services referral back in August, enquiring why five year old George didn't appear to be enrolled at a school. Fortunately she was au fait with the law and guidelines around elective home education (parents can legally choose to educate their children 'otherwise' than through attendance at a school), so the query was easy enough to answer.

I also have an update from journal entry 6. I finally had a response from Samaritans (so they had received my application; an automated acknowledgement at the time would have been helpful rather than internet silence), to say they had allocated their fifty London Marathon places and I had not been successful. Of course it doesn't matter now as I have Mark's place to run the marathon, although I am still waiting for postal confirmation of this nearly a month after I was assured a pack would be in the post. I think yet another email to the organisers may be required to check they have my address entered correctly. Meanwhile I shall continue to train, but more mindfully and a little less Gung-Ho. I don't want to scupper this running ship myself before it's even made it out onto the open seas of full-on marathon training.

Running Round the Park in Maternity Leggings

I have run 3-mile runs three times since my last entry, endeavouring to work on my ChiRunning technique and generally be more self-aware about the way I'm running. I am re-reading 'ChiRunning' at bedtime, well at least for as long as I can manage before I fall asleep and the book falls and hits me in the face. From what I've read so far, I think that last week's running niggles may have come from holding too much tension in my legs rather than achieving the relaxed stride I mentioned in the last chapter, also from trying to run too fast at the expense of good form.

My first two runs this week were great, I was running at the same pace as normal - between 9:30 and 9:45 minute miles - with much less effort, but my third run felt awful, I couldn't seem to relax into the running and was back to effort and discomfort again. I'm not really sure what made my experience different on that day; hopefully it was just an off day. As I'm sure all runners would agree, the dreaded 'off day' has a habit of striking without warning and often there is no identifiable reason why that day felt so much harder or more awkward than any other.

We've got as far as journal entry number 11, so it must be time to tell you the story of how I got into running at this point in my life. The story starts with my great friend Clare, the same age as me bar a few months in her favour, who I met in 1996 when we were in our mid-twenties and studying for a Diploma in Social Work at Bristol University. Since finishing that course, Clare has moved around the country for work, whilst I've mostly been having babies. In 2009 Clare came full circle, moving back to Bristol. Hooray! Crazy Clare (as she is sometimes called by my children, to distinguish her from the other Clares and Claires that we know) is sporadically given to taking part in athletic events and relying on gumption in place of training to complete the course (now you're seeing how she might have acquired her title). In the spring of 2010 Clare suggested that I join her in running the 10k Race for Life that June. I said yes, thinking it was high time I got fit again. Well, I have less natural gumption than Clare and knew I'd have to follow some kind of training schedule in preparation. I think we had about six weeks before the race, so I needed to get from zero active fitness to 10k-ready in that time. Setting aside her normal carefree approach, Clare decided to do some training with me too.

Our starting point was running laps around my local park. Actually saying 'laps' may be exaggerating a little; we ran three sides of the football pitch and walked one to begin with and the day we ambitiously tried to run two laps non-stop it nearly killed us. My attire probably looked hilarious, certainly in the eyes of the teenagers hanging out in the park anyway. I managed to find a pair of old trainers but I had no other sportswear so I had to make do with a very unflattering pair of old maternity leggings; not a good look. I had yet to discover the wonderful world of high-tech running gear or even the bargain end of that market where the general rule seems to be that the less you pay the more fluorescent your active wear will be.

I tried to run three times a week, either in the park with Clare or around the sports field while my kids were doing football club or swimming classes. I also aimed to swim once a week. I was so pleased with myself the first time I ran for twenty minutes without stopping, at least until my friend Mary pointed out that it would actually take me a least an hour to run a 10k. Oh. I think my longest run before the Race for Life was something like fifteen full laps of the park (the whole park not just the football pitch). I can't recollect now how long it took me or what I had estimated the distance to be equivalent to; unfortunately my brain is far too cluttered to retain that kind of non-essential information.

The big day arrived and I had something slightly closer to sportswear to put on and a decent pair of trainers. Looking back at the photos from that day however, I have to say that the outfit was not flattering in combination with the excess baby/busy mum/comfort eating weight I was carrying. Cringe. I got round the course in somewhere between 1:07 and 1:15 I think. The Race for Life not being an event with timing chips and not having thought to time myself or notice what the event clock said when I crossed the busy start line, that's as close as I can get to an approximate finish time. I felt disappointed that I had walked more than I'd hoped to during the race, but in retrospect I think I did pretty well considering I'd only been running for six weeks. A few weeks later, I spotted a poster advertising Bristol half-marathon that September and calculated that we had just enough time to train for it. Clare was up for the challenge, of course, and I've been running ever since. Yes, I caught the running bug.

But why do I stick with running now I'm in better shape? Why not choose aerobics, spin, Pilates, Zumba or the gym? I think the appeal is that running fits so well into a busy lifestyle. All that anyone needs is a reasonable pair of trainers and a convenient chunk of time, there is no need to be bound by the timetable at the sports centre or to take more money out of the already stretched family budget to pay for classes. I also think that the fitness benefits in relation to actual time spent running are greater than with other forms of sport I've tried in the past. Within a few weeks I could feel a significant improvement in the general strength of my body and my posture had improved, previously soft bits started to feel firm (well those that should do anyway) and my waist made an appearance for the first time in many years. Friends began to ask if I'd lost weight. I hadn't in fact shed even an ounce but I must have looked better for muscles being more toned. I subsequently realised that I wouldn't lose weight through running a few times a week; I'd have to bite the bullet and actually eat less. Boo. Wouldn't we all like to lose weight without having to do that? Running is probably harder than some of the other fitness activities I mentioned in terms of the amount of determination it takes to keep going when you're out of shape and it starts to hurt, but that's where signing up for an achievable race really helps to incentivise you to keep going. I don't think I would be on my way to running the London marathon without that original 10k goal. Thanks Crazy Clare.

Journal Entry 12 – 23rd November 2012

Confirmation Finally Arrives for Runner 18689

I am managing to consistently run three times a week now, generally around a three mile run each time. Progress and routine - tick. I am sticking to the three mile distance, as being able to comfortably run for thirty minutes four times a week is the recommended starting point for the sixteen week marathon training programme that I'll be commencing at the end of December taken from The Non-Runner's Marathon Trainer. Perhaps the very short runs seem a bit pathetic when 26.2 miles is the end goal, but I'm content to be taking the time to focus on good form at this foundation stage and I'm also being realistic that after four months off this year, between recovering from my two injuries, I have to take the time to get my base fitness back before starting marathon training in earnest. My aim is to get to the 21st April 2013 injury free and finish the marathon for Mark, definitely not to get ahead of myself at this stage and put that in jeopardy. To show that there is progression happening in my fitness, I can report that on my last run my average pace was 9:11 minute miles, which is sixteen seconds per mile faster than the next fastest time I've logged since I started running again at the end of September. I would say that the general effort level feels about the same and I can't yet figure out whether that will remain the case or whether by the end of December running three miles will feel easy. Does running ever feel easy? I will get back to you on that one further down the line.

The timing of my runs is somewhat haphazard at the moment, which sometimes means that they don't happen on the intended day. For example, today I forgot that Pete would be out this afternoon when I'd hoped to run, so without childcare my planned run had to be postponed to another day. I can see that I'm going to need to get more disciplined before the end of the year and start timetabling runs rather than starting the day or week with just a vague idea in my head of when they will happen, otherwise there's the real risk that they may not happen at all.

Postal confirmation of my marathon place has finally arrived, a month and a half and a handful of emails and phone calls after the date I expected. In fact two identical packs then arrived within two days (like the old saying about buses). So say hello to runner 18689. Woohoo! This has meant that, being absolutely sure that I have a place to run, we have been able to crack on with working out plans for accommodation in London over marathon weekend for myself, Pete, the children, my mum and Clare.

Myself, mum, my stepdad (Mark's dad) and Jelena were in London yesterday to join a Place2Be school project visit and Jelena brought the news that Mark, having deferred his place, had booked a hotel room in London for the marathon weekend in 2013 which she would like me to use. This is really fantastic news, particularly as the hotel is booked for three nights and is perfectly located for getting to the marathon start and also the marathon expo that I have to attend to register. Jelena hopes to be in London to support me too and can stay with friends. Cheaper rooms have now been booked for everyone else at the less glamorous but more affordable for us Travelodge in Clapham Junction.

The Place2Be visit was at a primary school in Brent, where the charity have been well established providing support to troubled children, their parents and the school staff for some years. It was a great insight into the work of the organisation and the positive impact it has in the lives of individuals, families and the school community. Two of the main impressions I came away with were the significance that support during childhood has for individuals experiencing emotional problems in terms of their success in education and their well being and mental health in adulthood (and I think the latter is why Mark may have chosen to support the work of Place2Be) and the location of support services within schools as an excellent way of improving uptake by those in real need. I am thrilled to be raising money for this charity through running the marathon and to have a better understanding now of exactly how the services are provided. I was also able to meet Jenny the fundraising coordinator in person and, as well as providing me with a Place2Be running top to wear for the marathon, she said they hoped to provide a presence to support me on the day which I was very touched by.

Journal Entry 13 – 2nd December 2012

Contemplating Some Interesting Parallels

I won't bore you with further details of my regime of three mile runs, but my simple routine has prompted me to contemplate some interesting parallels between marathon training plans and styles of home education. Stay with me on this one. To elaborate, this train of thought left the station after conversations with a friend from church, Graham, who is a similar age to myself and began running at around the same point in time. Here are our fact-files for comparative purposes:

Name: Andrea (aka Mum, Babe or Ands)
Age: 41
Running since: 2010
Race history: 10k, 4 half-marathons
Half-marathon PB: 2:12
Longest recent run: 5.5 miles
Marathon entered: London on 22nd April 2013
Length of marathon training plan: 16 weeks
Runs/week on training plan: 4
Cross-training: Highly unlikely

Longest training run on plan: 18 miles
Highest mileage training week: 35 miles

Name: Graham (aka Orgs, Big Org)
Age: Forty-something (more than 41)
Running since: 2010
Race history: 10k, 2 half-marathons
Half-marathon PB: 1:46
Longest recent run: 16 miles
Marathon entered: Taunton on 8th April 2013
Length of marathon training plan: 18 weeks
Runs/week on training plan: 6
Cross-training: Possibly
Longest training run on plan: 22 miles
Highest mileage training week: 55 miles

I have confidence that the plan I'm following has been tried and tested and is suitable for me to get through the training intact and complete a marathon. However, when I'm comparing training notes with Graham such is the difference in intensity, particularly in the earlier weeks, that it's a challenge to be honest about the low mileage I'm running at the moment; the temptation to exaggerate or be deliberately vague is surprisingly strong.

So, where do the parallels with styles of home education come in? If you talk to different families about why and how they home educate their children the answers will vary widely, from those, like myself, who choose a largely child-led approach (also known as unschooling or autonomous education) to those who have curriculums, timetables and workbooks galore and intend to cover all the traditional educational bases thoroughly. I guess it's obvious that one would choose a particular marathon training plan or method of home education over another on the basis of individual priorities and goals - as far as running is concerned, mine as an on and off runner, full time mum of four and home educator will naturally be different to Graham's as a committed runner and single man without a family - but the thing that interests me is that whilst I can clearly see the reasons for our differences, I still have to check that they don't become a source of anxiety. The fear comes from that tendency many of us have to compare ourselves with others and think, "Ooh, maybe I should be doing it like that instead. Maybe my approach is all wrong". I should know better than to worry about my training plan really, having spent the last eight years since my eldest child officially hit school age learning to follow my convictions about the validity of alternative methods of education. There is more than one way to successfully train for a marathon, just as there are many ways to raise a healthy, happy child. In both instances the proof will be in the pudding, but it's having the nerve to stay the course and not change tack out of fear, whilst also having the humility and courage to go in a new direction when there's a sound reason to do so.

To fill in the some gaps for you, as I'm sure you must be curious about my family and home education. My four children are, Sam who is 12, Keziah 10, Zoe 8 and George aged 5 and they have always been home educated. To clarify, the term home education, or home schooling, refers most accurately to the fact that the parents have chosen (as is their legal right) to maintain full responsibility for their child's education rather than giving that responsibility to a school. It does not mean that the children's education only happens within the confines of the family home - in fact my husband complains that we're hardly ever at home - or that children are isolated from other children. We are blessed to know a fantastic and very supportive network of home school families in Bristol. Our reasons for choosing to home educate are manifold, but to summarise them I would say that we believe that school is often not the best place for a child to grow into themselves and realise their individual potential, with the negative effects of peer pressure and too much of a one size fits all approach irrespective of an individual's learning style, interests, strengths and weaknesses.

I suspect that even if I were a stronger and more committed athlete, my marathon-training plan would still reflect my outlook on life. I would choose a plan that could deliver the desired result without being so intensive that the process of getting there might be miserable.

Journal Entry 14 – 29th December 2012

Christmas Comes and Goes and Training Commences in Earnest

It's been a while since I last wrote, so to bring things up to date here is what the last few weeks have contained: More singing rehearsals (this time working towards our church's Christmas carol concert), runs in the rain, two nights away in Torquay with Pete and without children (thank you mum and Living Social), making and sending cards before the last Christmas post (only just), Christmas parties, Christmas visits with relatives, runs in the wind in coastal Lincolnshire, late night wrapping sessions (not to be confused with late night rapping sessions, I've never been that cool), my first club night back at Sole Sisters for several months, Christmas home baking (home-made mincemeat for mince pies and my own experimental Christmas cake flavour fudge), a slightly niggly knee, Christmas shopping and Amazon orders, cracking the art of the early(ish) morning run (I have discovered that I can manage it as long as I have a cup of tea before I go and it doesn't involve getting out of bed before about 7.30 a.m. You got it, I'm really not a morning person) and, very importantly, two weeks completed on the marathon training programme. Phew...and breathe.

Thank goodness for time away over Christmas and New Year with Pete's lovely mum Sheila and stepdad Ken in Lincolnshire; time to relax away from the normal demands of life. How blessed we are to have family who can cope with a house invasion on our scale, having a spare bedroom, rooms that can double-up as bedrooms, lots of camp beds and masses of generosity and patience. Generally we visit three times a year for a week or so and it is always a thoroughly welcome time of rest and refreshment. If I want to run during our stay, there is a flat 3.3-mile loop from the house along country roads and through villages that serves me very well.

I decided to get a head start on the marathon training plan, feeling ready and fit to move on after working up to running four times a week, so I've started two weeks early but will be doubling up on each of the first two weeks of the plan so that by the fourth scheduled week of the plan I'll be where I would have been anyway (if you're following me). In theory, I could have allowed for two extra weeks near the end of the plan for additional long runs, but have decided that I would prefer to opt for easing into the plan more slowly. So, my running week is now and for the foreseeable future:

Monday - short run, working up to 5 miles.
Wednesday - medium run, working up to 8 miles.
Thursday - short run, working up to 5 miles.
Saturday - long run, working up to 18 miles.

The last two weeks have consisted of 3, 4, 3 and 5-mile runs. So far, so good. I am very happy to be able to say that I have mastered the art of running without requiring walking breaks. My lungs and legs are co-operating well thanks to putting in that time on building my base fitness, so now it's my mind that is most likely to rebel at the effort of staying focused and ensuring that one foot goes in front of the other in a manner that maintains good form. I can see that company on the long runs will help to make the experience more enjoyable by lightening things up, otherwise I think after three or more hours on my feet I might be finding the mental concentration more draining than the physical effort. I don't tend to run with music - which I know many people find an essential companion - as I find it too distracting, but I do need to find a good balance so that there is focus but I don't get mental burnout.

With reference to the slightly niggly knee I mentioned, it's a bit of a mystery and something that I'm hoping will clear up of it's own accord. If not, I'm sure you will be hearing more about it. I have had a little trouble with shin splints again too, so there are obviously some changes I need to make. I think my ChiRunning style is along the lines of a film inspired by a true story. In other words, I have taken elements from the technique that I can easily work with and that help me, but my style may be a quite a way from the genuine article. However, overall I'm really happy with how things are going and, importantly, I'm enjoying the running and not finding it a chore to do. I can already say that should my marathon journey not go any further, I am a stronger runner for the work I've put in up to this point, which is a satisfying achievement in itself.

I haven't got hold of any new running books to read yet, but I am discovering running magazines after dipping into a few recently in my dentist's waiting room and yesterday I purchased a copy of Running Fitness. This could become an addictive habit if my history of compulsively reading pregnancy magazines during each of my pregnancies is anything to go by. I'm not sure how much truly useful additional information I will gain through magazine articles, but they do enable me to saturate myself in running stories and information, and also make easy bedtime reading. I shall let you know which turns out to be my favourite. I think there are several more on the market to sample, off the top of my head I'm aware of Runner's World and Women's Running magazines. Having mentioned visiting the dentist, I can't let the opportunity pass without taking the opportunity to lament one of the many signs of ageing that I've started to experience in the last few years, namely the requirement for more dental work. Gone are the days when I could say that I've only ever had one filling, instead I'm becoming familiar with hygienists and root fillings (thankfully only one of those so far). And while I'm on the subject of teeth, why does more food get stuck in-between your teeth as you get older? What is that all about? I can appreciate now why some people like to have a toothpick to hand after a meal. More age-related observations may follow.

Journal Entry 15 – 11th January 2013

More Miles and More Magazines

I have six miles to run tomorrow on my training schedule and I am actually looking forward to it. At the beginning of this journey I said I liked the results of running but I wasn't crazy about the process, but that is definitely changing as I get stronger. Retrospectively, I can see that what I've called training for a race has only been half the job, or less sometimes. Making the commitment to follow a programme one hundred percent, as I have this time, is a totally different fitness experience. As I wrote in my last entry, I can now run and keep running, the miles feel shorter and I step out of the door for a run feeling positive rather than beating back mild feelings of dread. Also, and this is a complete first for me, in the last mile of a 5.2 mile run with Sole Sisters at the beginning of this week, I spontaneously broke into a sprint. My body is definitely way ahead of my mind on that one.

On a less positive note, I have continued trying to work out why I have discomfort on the inside of my left knee - not normally when I am running, but on and off in between runs - and mild shin splints, as these are new problems. I've not had them as a result of running before. The ChiRunning book says it should be possible to resolve discomfort and injuries by working on good form, the premise being that running injuries don't have to be inevitable as you rack up the miles if you can avoid placing undue strain on the body by giving it the optimum conditions to work well. My latest attempts to get to the bottom of these niggles are a pair of new trainers (worth a try) and speeding up my cadence. I'll return to that piece of running jargon in a minute.

As I mentioned before, I haven't run hundreds of miles in my previous trainers yet and they still feel fine, but I've begun to wonder if trainers with less structure and not such a built up heel might be worth trying, particularly as I'm running with a midfoot strike not heel-striking. From my foray into the world of running magazines and ChiRunning, I have discovered that foot strike during running is becoming widely recognised as an important factor in the reduction of stress on joints and the promotion of a more natural running form. In my history of buying new running shoes so far - I'm currently on my fifth pair - I haven't yet spent more than around £55. Neither have I been for gait analysis in a specialist running shop. Expensive trainers - which for me is a pair costing over £60 - are beyond my budget, so a discount shop like Sports Direct is where I would normally look. This time I have found something that seems like it may fit the bill in T K Maxx (another discount store, for those not au fait with the world of cut-price shopping), spending a meagre £29.99. My advice for choosing trainers, beyond making sure they're a comfortable fit and give your feet support where you naturally feel like you need it, is to make sure you have plenty of room around your toes even if that means going for a larger size than you would normally choose in shoes. I now go for a UK size 6 even though I've never worn a shoe or trainer larger than a 5 before. Obviously you need to make sure they still fit well particularly around the heel, we're not aiming for sloppy clown shoes, but the extra toe room - enough to be able to wiggle in and so that your toes are not touching the end of the trainer at all - means that your feet can work well in their full range of movement without being cramped and also means that you won't get black and bruised toenails when you do long races as I did the first time I did a half-marathon. The author of ChiRunning suggests that your running shoes should feel as comfortable as a pair of slippers, although I'd recommend aiming for a look with less tartan and without the Velcro fastenings.

Cadence refers to the speed of your leg turnover or how many strides one takes per minute. In the ChiRunning book, a cadence of 170-180 strides a minute is recommended. This can be worked on by running with a small clip-on metronome set to the speed you're aiming for. It stands to reason that a slower cadence equals more time per stride that the feet and legs are in contact with the ground and hence absorbing impact forces, and so a faster cadence lends itself more to a lighter footfall. I made a very feeble attempt at working on this a couple of years back and have been skipping over that section of the book ever since, but I was running a few days ago and praying for a solution to my niggles and I suddenly had the thought that cadence was the thing to focus on. For the last mile of that run I experimentally stepped up my cadence and again on my run the next day (that time with the metronome to help), and I have definitely had less knee discomfort and none at all in my shins since. Interesting. It's too early to say definitively if this is the answer, but I will continue to be mindful when I'm running and I'm sure I will soon know if there are other areas I need to work on besides.

So talking about answered prayer begs the question, does God take an interest in all the details of our lives including the very practical, nitty gritty and apparently non-spiritual areas? If you're interested in a Christian perspective, read Psalm 139, because I believe it shows that God knows us personally and intimately on every level, better than we know ourselves in fact, and therefore is our perfect advisor and physician. I remember talking during my friend Anne's hen weekend to a work colleague of hers and telling her the story of how a group of Christian friends had prayed for Anne, who was then in her early 30s and starting to fret that it might never happen, to meet a husband and how we were all now witnesses to those prayers having been answered (and in an amazing way, but that's not really my story to share). Anne's colleague was surprised at me making a connection between Anne meeting her soon-to-be husband Rob and answered prayer, she said she didn't realise that God could be petitioned so specifically. I believe that he can and indeed that he desires to be, the only caveat being that our prayers will be answered in line with God's character and his understanding of what we need which is not always the same as what we think we need.

I have now purchased and read copies of Women's Running and Running Fitness as well as Runner's World and, yes, I think this may become a monthly habit for the duration of my marathon training, quite an expensive one though. I have enjoyed reading all of them and they all have articles that I would go back to and read again, which is more than can be said for many magazines. I couldn't choose an obvious favourite yet, but I would say that Women's Running is maybe more accessible for someone like myself who isn't ever likely to be considered a serious runner by those who would consider themselves to be so (I hark back to that sentence from 'Run Less, Run Faster' in an earlier chapter). Frustratingly I now have to wait a week or so for next month's copies so I'll have to read them more slowly in the future. Perhaps I should ration myself to two articles an evening.

Journal Entry 16 – 23rd January 2013

Snow and Ice, a Touch of Flu and Losing My Running Mojo

This has been a week of new experiences, some highs and some lows.

I had my first ever experience of running on snow and ice, followed a few days later by slush, puddles and mud - much less fairytale. I had decided to join the other Sole Sisters who are marathon training for London, Manchester and Brighton marathons for their long run on Saturday morning and this, as it turns out, was a good call because there is no weather system that stops the Sisters from running and I would have been nervous to venture out in the snow and ice on my own and might otherwise have ended up hanging up my trainers for that weekend. I was scheduled to run seven miles on my own training plan, but ended up running closer to ten miles to fit in with what the rest of the group were doing. It was an exhilarating experience, the snow having worked its magic in transforming every leaf and twig into a picture of breathtaking beauty, and after the first tentative paces on the crunchy, icy surface of the Bristol to Bath cycle path - which follows the path of an old railway line - it became apparent that it was actually fairly safe to run on in comparison to the smoother and more treacherous ice on the frequently trodden pavements elsewhere. I could feel that I was having to run a little differently to usual on this new surface and I anticipated some aches and pains the following day, but as it turned out they were thankfully mild, just some stiffness at the top of my legs.

I now find myself with something of a conundrum though because, whilst it was really great to have company on a long run, I would prefer to learn to run straight through and Sole Sisters runs always involve quite a few stops to regroup, spend a penny, chat, etc. Forgive the stereotype, but it is a women's running club. I don't know whether the stops reduce the overall endurance benefit of the run compared to running straight through - possibly they don't - but my concern is that to always train in this way on my long runs would leave me psychologically unprepared for race day when I'm not planning on stopping every few miles. So, I think my feeling is that the benefits of company on the longer runs will have to be balanced with my desire to prepare as well as I can for marathon day both physically and mentally. There may be some lonely miles ahead for me; hopefully they'll be character building ones though.

The second new experience is that having felt largely positive along my marathon journey so far, sometime in between that long snowy run and a touch of flu mid-week (which meant I missed my first run since starting the marathon training programme), I temporarily lost my running mojo. It laced up its trainers and ran off in the opposite direction. Humph. I suddenly felt overwhelmed at the thought of all the miles I have yet to cover in training and I began to question whether I really have what it takes to complete the programme let alone the actual marathon at the end of it. The size and loneliness of the task loomed far larger than they ever have before and I felt scared. After a chat over a coffee with Clare and some time reminding myself how far I've come since I started, I think I'm getting back on track. Some of my fear comes from the prospect of tackling long training runs on my own, which I concede is a self-inflicted prospect as I could enjoy the company of the lovely Sole Sisters. My desire to be prepared the best I can be for marathon day and my own interpretation of what that preparation looks like I find pulls me in another direction though. Perhaps I can take some inspiration for the long lonely runs by remembering that Mark always ran alone. I'm trying really hard not to give in to the temptation to break with the advice in the Non-Runner's Marathon Trainer and mentally set myself a target race finish time - and it does still count as a transgression if I have a time in my mind, even if I never allow myself to say it out loud - but in truth I would like to do a bit more than aiming to finish. I'd like my effort to be a respectable one for my age and fitness level, which in translation means I'd like to run as much of the way round as I can and not to finish in a time that can only be mumbled behind my hand. Am I setting my sights too high? We will find out in 12 weeks time.

My touch of flu (and it was just a touch, I was able to get through a normal day I just would have loved a duvet day but that doesn't really happen when you have children unless you're nearly at death's door) I guess means that my streak of running-induced immunity has come to an end. I had a mild cold over Christmas too. I would still say that overall I'm definitely enjoying much better resistance to the bugs that do the rounds since taking up running. I could probably do with getting more sleep to stay on top form, which brings me to the list of things I think I need to give attention to over the next 12 weeks. The list is currently:

- Go to bed by midnight (possibly not tonight though as it's 11.45 already).

- Practice good hydration during my long runs (very important as I normally prefer to run without water but I've read that good hydration is one of the keys to a successful marathon).

- Work out my race pace for running the marathon, particularly the first half, and practice running at this pace on my long runs.

- Decide whether or not to use energy gels on race day. If I decide that I will, practice using them on my long runs.

- Introduce some cross training for core strength and working on key muscle groups.

I'm not sure I'll manage the last item on the list and the first is going to take considerably more resolve than I'm displaying right now (it's 00.21), but the rest will happen.

I've realised that I could easily plough through all the training without actively including my children in the process, so, with this in mind, I looked up the origins of marathon running on YouTube the other day and we found out about Pheidippides. Keziah was interested but the younger two raised a cry of "Boring!" I have also made a wall chart of my remaining training runs for the kitchen, so that the children can cross them off as they're done, see how far I'm running and get a better picture of the build-up to the big day and all that entails. Up to now the extent of the children's involvement has been me coming down the stairs in my running gear at regular intervals during the week to wails of "Oh, you're not going running again are you?" Realistically I may still get that, but hopefully it will be tempered with some understanding of what it's all heading towards. I may need to make a rota to say whose turn it is to cross off the run on the chart though or there will be strife. Is there actually anything kids will not fight over?

Journal Entry 17 – 29th January 2013

Running into Double Digits at Last

This week's training runs are 3, 5, 3 and 10 miles. I must be over last week's wobble because I'm looking forward to the long run. It will feel like a landmark to get into double digits after four months of running. I probably could have tackled a ten mile run long before now, having run that distance in training for half-marathons before (admittedly with stops), but it might have felt miserable, whereas at this point I'm confident that I can run it and feel strong throughout. Last weekend's long run was eight miles - I did it on my own straight through - and I found it helpful to think that a marathon is that distance times three plus a bit. Yes, really, I actually found that helpful, it made it easier to visualise the 26.2 miles so that now it feels a little less abstract and, dare I say it yet, more manageable.

To give an idea of how the runs fit into my week and into family life, Monday runs I do with Sole Sisters in the evening, the rest I normally do alone, ideally first thing in the morning, although, as I've already confessed, my first thing is normally about 8.30am so not mega-early. Practically speaking, I have discovered it works much better to run at the beginning of the day and it's a great feeling to have my run already in the bag as I head into the rest of the day rather than starting out worrying when and whether it can be squeezed in around our other commitments. I lay the table for breakfast the night before so the children can be getting on with that while I'm out and, fortuitously for me at least, Pete is signed off work for the time being so I'm not having to fit running around his work hours in order to make sure he can be at home with the children while I go out running.

Monday runs are longer than the three miles my training programme specifies at this point, as club night run distances start at a minimum of four miles. To break with the plan even more - what a rebel - I've been opting to go above the four and run with the five-mile group so that the group matches the speed I'm comfortable to run at. Next week I might run with the fast six mile group though because last Monday I got a bit too far ahead with the fives and they couldn't call me back when I went the wrong way. Fortunately we were nearly at the end and I knew where I was so I couldn't go too far wrong and get lost. Although I'm doing more miles on club nights than I technically need to, we stop and start so I can use it as an opportunity to do a different kind of training to usual. Once I'm warmed up I can do some of the sections at a faster speed than I would normally run knowing that the longest section will probably not be further than 1.5 miles. What kind of run does that count as? Threshold, tempo, interval? I don't know. I find all the terminology rather confusing, as the different types of run seem to overlap. Last time I did one section at eight-minute mile pace, which is fast for me, and it felt great. We also ran up a good few hills so that will have training benefits too.

When I'm going out for a run alone, I always run from my front door and there are several main roads that I can follow to take me off in different directions and add variety. I used to avoid some roads if they undulated too much (a clever choice of word that is used in race descriptions if the course is not really flat but equally doesn't include any very nasty hills), but I can take the undulations and even the occasional nasty hill in my stride now, so north Bristol is my oyster in theory if not in practice. Aren't we all such creatures of habit? All my running is on hard pavements, which I know is not advised as it inflicts the most wear and tear on the body, but going off-road would involve a whole new set of calculations about where to go and personal safety which at the moment feels too much to take on.

An update post - long run:

My 10 mile run was completed in 1:33. I think I can safely say that's a personal best for me (smiley face emoji). Graham and I finally got round to arranging to run together, having talked about it for a year or so. I ran 2.5 miles to the end of his road, we then went straight into 6.5 miles together, and then I took a shorter route home for the final mile. The 6.5 mile section was the fastest, we clocked around 8:45 mile pace in some parts. Graham insisted that I was setting the pace and he was following my lead, so I imagine that knowing I was running with someone who normally runs at a faster pace than myself, I automatically then stepped-up mine. I was aware that I was pushing myself but it didn't feel uncomfortable, not until afterwards anyway. The distraction of company and chat - yes, amazingly I did still have enough breath to chat - definitely helped me to push myself beyond my normal comfort zone. For the rest of the day I was physically exhausted though, if the day had allowed for it I would have gone for a lie-down, not to sleep but just to allow all my weary muscles to fully relax. The day in question being Pete's birthday, a lie-down didn't factor in the equation. There was birthday cake to be baked - at least supervision and assistance required while Sam baked - and a homemade birthday present to be hastily finished before Keziah went off to a friend's birthday party, as well as all the usual meals to be cooked for the family, etc., etc. I did manage to sneak in a post-run self-congratulatory pot of tea and a Panini in a coffee shop after I dropped Keziah at the party (another smiley face emoji). The next day I was somewhat stiff in the hips but my overall recovery wasn't as big a deal as the previous day's aches might have led me to believe it would be. Clare is cautioning me not too push myself too hard and run the risk of injury before London and I think she has a point. I know that running faster occasionally will benefit my overall fitness and performance but there is a probably a balance to be found with staying injury free in the run up to the marathon.

The first week of my final twelve counting down to marathon day has been completed and I have 4 green 'I did it' stickers on my wall chart. 11 weeks to go.

Journal Entry 18 – 12th February 2013

I Have a Bit of a Scare, Run up a Very Steep Hill and Start Fundraising

4, 5, 4 and 11 mile runs were on my schedule for this week and have been successfully completed, meaning I now have two rows of green 'I did it' stickers on the training chart in the kitchen. My daughter Keziah commented that it didn't feel like the chart had been up for long, yet I was working through it really quickly. For me, the still-to-be-run rows are making a much bigger statement. I think I need to tip over the half way mark before I'll start to feel satisfied with the quantity of green sticker coverage. We also have some red stickers to put on for missed runs to shame me into sticking to the plan and my Thursday four mile run box did get a red sticker temporarily as I skipped it thinking I had pulled a muscle. Amazingly after a day off I felt absolutely fine, so I did the run on Friday instead and we could replace the red sticker with a green one. Disgrace duly averted. Feeling enough pain to think I'd done something serious was quite a scare. Although I have mentioned a few niggles to date, this was the first time I really thought I'd need to stop training for a while. Bizarrely, having resigned myself to missing some runs, even the possibility that, like Mark, I might not actually make it to marathon day fit to run, what felt like a bad muscle pull in my groin put itself completely right in less than twenty four hours. Go figure. As I've often thought whilst going through my four pregnancies, it's a strange thing to inhabit your body full time yet have so little idea what's going on inside it. Needless to say, I am breathing huge sighs of relief that all appears to be ok and two runs, one of them being the eleven miles, seems sufficient to be sure that all is in good working order. The knee problem and shin splints that I've mentioned before also seem to have resolved, so I'm pleased to say that I'm feeling fit and ready for the intense training yet to come.

In terms of the average pace I'm now running at, my Monday evening run with Sole Sisters I decided to make a deliberately slow four mile recovery run (instead of the six I thought I might go for) after pushing myself on the long ten mile run with Graham a few days before, but my other runs during the week I ran at around 9:20 minute mile pace. That's the same pace as I ran with Graham, so it seems to be where I naturally settle at the moment unless I'm having a tired day or have run up too many hills and worn myself out.

Speaking of hills, today on the eight-mile portion that I ran with Graham out of my total of eleven miles, I was introduced to the long hill (just short of a mile) that he and his running friend Nick have nicknamed 'The Tock' (Tockington Hill). That is one mean hill, particularly the final few hundred metres. Phew! The hill slowed me down considerably although I did make it to the top without walking, so my average pace for that particular run worked out at 9:45 minute miles which I'm still really happy with for a long run. All of the long runs I've done over the last month or so are territory I haven't revisited since training for and running Bath half-marathon in March 2012. In fact arguably since I'm now running without stops for the first time ever, this is completely new running territory, so I'm really happy with the progress that I've made in terms of speed and strength through making a commitment to following a training plan diligently. My race pack has arrived in the post for this year's Bath half-marathon on March 3rd and I am looking forward to finding out whether my marathon training has improved my performance in a half. I am definitely hoping to run my first half-marathon without walking stops and, of course, hoping to improve on my time. Running 2:05 would be good (a seven minute improvement); 2:00 straight would be amazing! Go on, organise a quick sweepstake before you read that entry.

Having spent a bit of time here and there since Christmas putting my JustGiving marathon fundraising page together to collect donations for Place2Be, this week I shared the link with my Facebook friends and, thanks to a few generous donors, I have already raised 13% of my £1000 target. I'm hoping by emailing family and friends individually, to come within reach of the fundraising target fairly quickly. Although marathon running is becoming more popular, I'm optimistic that the undertaking still carries enough kudos to help people get past any charity giving fatigue they might feel to dig deep and make a donation. The proliferation of charity sporting events is great for the causes that benefit, but as a participant it can feel awkward to keep asking the same circle of supporters to donate time and again. Charities often encourage participants to think of imaginative ways of fundraising to get round this giving-fatigue and help people part willingly with their hard earned cash, but I haven't yet engaged my creativity in this area, it requiring extra energy and brainpower to that currently at my disposal. My brain is definitely stretched to full capacity at present, as evidenced by my worrying inability to mentally synch events. I am very likely to have two or more family activities on the same day and totally omit to work out how they will interlink in terms of timing and travel until the moment is upon me and it's all gone horribly wrong. It doesn't help that I have some things written on the kitchen calendar, some on my mobile phone's calendar (which I now can't read properly since the phone got dropped and the screen broke), some on emails and some in my head.

I haven't bought any more running magazines since my Christmas splurge, but I have bought a 'magbook' - does that mean it's more than a magazine but not quite a book? - about marathon training (quite useful) and also one of the books I'd had my eye on for a while, Phil Hewitt's 'Keep on Running - The Highs and Lows of a Marathon Addict'. I read Phil's account of his twenty-five or so marathons (to date) compulsively. It was a good read, despite not finding a lot in it to relate to on a personal level. I think it highly unlikely that I will go on to become a marathon addict myself; one will probably suffice. Plus I think the experience of a fairly serious male runner - even with having the young family element in common with myself - is significantly different to my own. The roles of wife and mother (in my situation at least) come with different constraints and expectations to those of husband and father. I have been given somewhat grudging acceptance of the hours of running time required to make training for this marathon possible but it's been quite a big adjustment for Pete and the kids to get used to me spending so much time away from them doing something for myself and if I wanted to make a habit of running on this scale I think I would meet with resistance. So, in that respect, Phil Hewitt's freedom to pursue his marathon ambitions at home and round the globe is simultaneously enviable and alien. However, despite my inability to connect with Phil's narrative, I think Mark would have identified strongly with the following quote from the book:

> 'It was the extremeness of marathon running which appealed, which was possibly in itself a reflection of my more than modest record in PE at school.... The low point came at the end of my second summer at secondary school when school report time came round...C+ for attainment, C+ for effort...Even worse was the comment: 'It is felt that Philip is somewhat lacking in co-ordination.'.... I wouldn't pretend that the slight altered the course of

my life.... But maybe, just maybe, the put-down was there, lurking somewhere unacknowledged at the back of my mind, in the marathons I was now doing. It would be wrong to suggest that I was trying to prove something to a games teacher who had long since forgotten me, but possibly the memory heightened my satisfaction when I discovered I could indeed compete at the upper end of the sporting scale. I had gone off and got a degree. I had even completed a doctorate. And now I was turning on the sporting prowess. I was one of the boys - at last.'

Journal Entry 19 – 16th February 2013

Reaching Marathon Training Midpoint and I Unofficially Beat My Half-Marathon PB

4, 6, 4 and 12 miles runs were on the schedule for last week but I ran 6, 4, 6 and 13.67 miles. Just a modicum of rebellion there. It was again a mixed experience as a training week, engendering both confidence and concerns but finishing on a high note with a reasonably solid long training run comfortably inside my previous fastest time over the half-marathon distance of 13.1 miles. I took six minutes off without obviously pushing myself and that includes running up another serious hill. Thank you Graham. Take that sarcastically or genuinely; either could apply depending on whether we're referring to monstrous hills or supportive partnership through those long miles.

I began the week by running with the fast six-mile group at Sole Sisters club night, the first time I've done that for a while. It went well, but was too far and too fast to qualify as the recovery run it was supposed to be. On Wednesday I swapped my scheduled six miles for four, as it was my younger daughter Zoe's ninth birthday and I didn't want to be out for too long. Those four miles felt like ridiculously hard work and I was very thankful that I didn't have the extra two miles to run. For the first mile or so it was snowing, but it didn't turn out to be as romantic to run through the snow as I had imagined it would be because it turns out that the stuff gets in your eyes and is quite uncomfortable - ski goggles would have been helpful.

On Thursday I dithered over whether to run four or six miles as I'd already done a six on Monday, but decided it would be good to do six straight through without stops. Again it felt like a real push, probably due to fatigue from my last long run coupled with Monday's fast six. In the last few miles I started to feel some discomfort above my left ankle between the front and inside of my leg and also on the inside of the same knee. I'd had some stiffness in the knee after my last long run but nothing at all after Monday or Wednesday's runs. Perhaps I should have stopped and walked, but I chose to finish the run. Afterwards those areas felt really stiff and uncomfortable, I wouldn't go so far as to say painful though, and the frustration kicked in from feeling great one day then finding myself nursing another new niggle the next. For the following two evenings I did the ginger treatment and worried about my long run coming up at the weekend. Some people seem to advise taking time off from running as soon as you feel an injury or sense the potential for one, even if just a couple of days, others seem to suggest carrying on but being mindful about how you are running, plus considering other factors like your trainers, running surface, etc. It's so hard to know which advice to take when you're following a training schedule with a race date creeping ever closer on the calendar. The ginger definitely seemed to help though and by Saturday I was confident that I could at least give the long run a go and stop if necessary.

Long run Saturday dawned dry and bright - thankfully I haven't had to run in the rain recently, just snow - and I had been persuaded by my now established partner, long run Graham, to attempt fourteen miles instead of the twelve on my schedule so that I could go over the magical 13.1 mile half-marathon distance for the first time ever. The running for the first eight miles was great and felt very comfortable, then we hit a big hill on a path winding up to the Dower House overlooking the M32 on the outskirts of Bristol. After the hill I felt considerably less fresh and the rest of the run felt like hard work. The area above my left ankle started to feel a bit stiff during the last three miles, but I found that if I consciously relaxed my lower leg as it swung through for the next stride rather than flexing my foot upwards, it felt much better. I reached 13.1 miles in 2:06:26 and felt totally spent. Instead of rounding up to a tidy fourteen miles, I stopped and walked at 13.67 when I was just round the corner from Graham having gone separate ways to run back to our respective homes. Sshh, don't tell. I was a bit stiff in my ankle and knees for the rest of that day, but much less the next day and by Monday I felt fine. So, a good recovery I would say. I did make sure I stretched really well after the run including trying a few new stretches from my marathon training magbook, maybe that helped.

Yesterday on the next Sole Sisters club night, I took it nice and steady choosing five miles instead of six to try and make it a proper slow recovery run and all was functioning well physically. Hopefully I can relegate last week's worries to the passing niggles category rather than upgrading them to potential injuries to keep an eye on.

Apart from working through the miles, other marathon related activities and happenings include confirming my hotel room for marathon weekend - thank you Jelena for getting Mark's booking transferred to my name, The Hilton at Canary Wharf looks a bit posh in comparison to my usual Travelodge hotel experience - booking train travel up to London and receiving an email from Place2Be who have noticed that my Just-Giving page is up and running and starting to generate some donations for them. Place2Be's fundraising manager, Jenny, expressed the charity's appreciation that my page was active and money was coming in for them already and offered to send my charity running T shirt and any fundraising materials I could use. So now, a few days later, I have a great Place2Be technical T-shirt to run the marathon in, four cotton T-shirts for the kids and some badges and things for my support team to wave on marathon day. I am, it could be said, excessively excited about my technical T-shirt because it's pretty stylish as charity tops go. I have run a few half-marathons in a fairly hideous and totally unflattering charity running vest so this will feel like the height of running fashion in comparison. Yes, I know, I may be getting a little carried away, it's only a T shirt and sadly 'technical' only refers to the sweat-wicking fabric that it's made of it doesn't mean it will somehow magically enhance my performance. Shame.

As far as the act of running goes and how I am feeling about it at this point in time, I must confess that I'm still not really sure if I actually like it. I love the fitness and body sculpting benefits running brings and the progression I've made since starting in 2010, and particularly since starting my marathon training, but I'm not sold on the process. Does that mean I never will be? I keep hoping to hit the point where running feels easier, maybe even to discover the mystical 'flow' that I've read about where it feels almost effortless, but instead I seem to be stuck in a place where putting one foot in front of another through miles and for hours just feels like sheer hard work. It feels hard and it goes on feeling hard until I stop. It's not like aerobics, which I did a lot of in the 90s (does anyone do aerobics anymore?), where you might do a hard move for a couple of minutes but you know you'll get a break after that set and hopefully the next move will be easier or, at the very least, hard in a different way using a different group of muscles. When I'm running my legs pretty quickly start to tell me that I'm asking them to do something they'd rather not, "We'd really rather be walking if it's all the same to you", they say, and they don't shut up about it until I stop. Clare tells me it's because I'm always pushing myself to run further and faster. That could be true. Since I started my marathon training at the end of September 2012 I've probably taken fifteen to twenty seconds off my average minutes per mile pace and will normally run some miles out of any given run at under nine minutes (and under by quite a lot on occasion). Maybe it's just that the flow is still to come, still to be experienced. Or maybe this gloom is symptomatic of all the training miles I've run to date and those still to be run. This is intense. I would love to love the act of running and maybe I will discover that in myself one day, but, in the meantime, I think perhaps the answer is to start paying more attention to the mental side of my marathon training. Perhaps my mind might find gainful employment keeping the protests of my body in check, rather than being their willing mouthpiece.

A Breakthrough
and I Kiss the Tarmac

I have completed my first ever sixteen mile run and, maybe more significantly, I enjoyed it. From the ashes of my muscle aching, training weary despondency, I have risen like a Lycra-clad phoenix. I could have stopped after fourteen miles but I chose (note that word, 'chose') to do two more and hit the sixteen miles that Graham and I had agreed on before we set out and prior to a sore calf muscle leading him to decide to cut his own run short that day. Just to reiterate and for absolute clarity, I will say it again. After running fourteen miles, I chose to run two more, even though I only had fourteen to do on my schedule this week. How about that for a turn around? Mind you, a little of the self-congratulatory wind was taken out of my sails at fifteen miles when two other marathon training Sole Sisters ran effortlessly past me looking as fresh as daisies on their own sixteen mile run. I comforted myself by deciding that they couldn't possibly be as far into their run as I was into mine at that point.

That sixteen miles was a great run for me. Yes I had moments of weariness, particularly during the interminable hills, but I recovered and found the run comfortable overall. The experience has really helped me to believe that, having completed the remainder of my training, I will be able to get round the marathon course without dragging myself through the second half feeling miserable. It has also been an encouragement to see that all these months of training are now bearing fruit. In terms of the running, I was getting closer to a flow experience; I'd say I touched the edges of flow. My recovery was good too, as it has been generally since starting the longer runs. I had some aches and stiffness for the rest of that day, much less the next day, and by Monday I was fine. It is simultaneously odd and fantastic that such a great experience should come immediately after my slump. I wonder if this is something that others have experienced on their own marathon journeys? Possibly it is as I've just read this passage in The Non-Runner's Marathon Trainer about hitting a trough in marathon training.

'We called this chapter "Crossing the Emotional Plateau" because it has been our experience that this week in the training [they were writing about the equivalent training week to the one that would have come after my blip, so very much around the same point] *is often a very difficult one for the people who have taken our class. It is your ninth week of training [out of a sixteen week program]. You're going to exceed 30 miles this week for the first time. You are going to go 16 miles this weekend! And you look at the training program for the next couple of weeks and you are going to go 16 miles again the next two weekends, and you still have seven weeks of training to go....and....and....and. For many people, it is a sort of flat spot. You've come a really long way, but you still have a long way to go'.*

I guess my mid-schedule misery was not out of the ordinary at all then. It's good to know I'm on track in every sense.

The weather continues to be very cold, but thankfully mostly dry. I seem to have found a combination of layers and accessories that work well for me so that I don't feel cold once I'm running and warmed up, but also I don't overheat. I have a pair of winter-weight Nike running tights from the swap shop at Sole Sisters that I love. In fact I love them even more since I ran in an alternative lighter weight pair the other day when the Nikes were sitting wet in the washing machine and I realised, as I shivered at the start of the run in the alternative pair, that not once have my legs felt at all cold in them no matter what the temperature. Up top I wear a similar weight long sleeve top with a high neck, over that a close fitting fleece body warmer (or gilet as Clare would say but I can't bring myself to because it sounds too pretentious) which also has a high neck and a hood, then I have a lightweight windproof running jacket (I'm not sure if it's meant to be water-proof too but it definitely isn't) and finally a high-viz sleeveless jacket (it could be described as another gilet if I must) which has very useful pockets for gloves, keys, tissues, energy gels, etc. When the cold is biting, I also wear running gloves and a head-band that is designed to cover the ears.

Stepping out of the house is the worst bit when it's somewhere between zero and four degrees Centigrade, as it has been a lot re-cently, but once I get running it's fine and it can actually be invig-orating to be breathing in the cool air as I run and feeling it on my face. When I start to feel too hot, I find that if I remove my gloves and headband that's enough and I don't need to peel off any other layers of clothing, which is great because it means I don't then have the rigmarole of having to tie items of spare clothing around my waist. In terms of how much (or little) needs to be spent on running gear, this outfit demonstrates that it can be done very cheaply. The running tights, being a swap amongst Sole Sisters without an obligation to give an item in exchange, were free. The long sleeve Shock Absorber brand top and high-viz Run 365 jacket Clare bought me at a car boot sale. The (rather posh for me) Ron Hill running jacket was a birthday present from Pete that we bought together at a sale in a department store. The fleece Asics body-warmer I bought years ago in Asda for not very much. The running gloves my mum bought me from Lidl. And finally, the

Karrimor headband was from Sports Direct for about a fiver. I am only mentioning all the labels and brands to show that you can pick up recognised makes for little or nothing and also that you can choose lesser known or chain store running wear and still get gear that looks fine and performs well. I might not be wearing the height of running fashion I grant you, but the clothing has proved itself functional over this cold winter and, being cash-strapped, I'll happily settle for that.

After my sixteen-mile milestone run - and did I remember to mention that I've never actually run that far before, ever? - the following week was spent training in preparation for Bath half-marathon. I ran 4.5 miles with Sole Sisters on the Monday, 8.5 miles with Graham on Wednesday evening, and 4 miles by my-self on Friday. After having told several people about the Sole Sister who took a tumble during our run on Monday - thank-fully she was fine, but she did put a few small holes in her run-ning tights - on Wednesday I then did the same thing myself. One second I was running to the edge of the kerb to cross at a junction, the next I was heading towards the pavement and an-ticipating the shock of hitting the hard surface. Fortunately I stood up with cuts, bruises and a scuff on my Garmin and no sprains or broken bones. I think Graham got more of a shock than I did in actually falling when he heard the huge wallop be-hind him and realised what had happened. I got on with the rest of the run and saved the full inspection of my wounds until I got home. I may have a little more sympathy next time one of my kids skins their knees as mine stung for ages, I mean literally for days. And now I have to practice what I preach and not pick my scabs. There are no holes in my precious Nike running tights though. Phew. They are obviously made of tough stuff. Cold re-sistant and pavement resistant - maybe they would have been worth paying full price for.

Journal Entry 21 – 5th March 2013

I Officially Smash My Half-Marathon PB!

I ran Bath half-marathon in 2:01:25 taking eleven minutes off my previous PB! (Several smiley face emojis in a row). I have never physically pushed myself so hard for so long, I really didn't know that I had that in me. True to my previous experiences with running half-marathons, the running felt tough from early in the race and I started to think that I might have to go into plod mode - which is what I call it when I am still running but slowly, heavily and just to make it round - but I had Graham running with me at his comfortable marathon pace and really wanting to help me do well, so somehow I managed to dig deep and keep going at a good pace. It turned out that I had more physical strength and endurance in me than I expected thanks to all the marathon training, and, together with the courage that I managed to muster to go for it and not cop-out, I was amazed to find that I can run fast - relatively speaking of course - for quite a long time. That may well be my peak half-marathon experience but, if that turns out to be the case, I'm content for it to be so. According to our Garmins, we actually ran an extra 0.2 of a mile, which could be partially accounted for by us having to weave in and out of other runners on the busy course, so a straight 13.1 miles would have put me a shade under two hours which is better than I have ever hoped for from myself. My Garmin put my overall average pace at 9:07 minute miles but the first few miles were slow because the course was so busy and we had started right at the back after a very last minute toilet stop, so probably my average pace once we got motoring along was even quicker. I really ran this one! I have always boggled at the front-runners steaming along and thought 'How do they do that for thirteen miles?' but I think I had the teeniest glimpse into that possibility, which feels like quite something for a forty one year old, started-late-in-life, part-time runner.

My primary lesson from this for London is that I will need to run a lot slower, because at the pace I ran Bath there is no way that I could have gone much farther, I certainly couldn't have doubled the distance. So my task now is to identify my comfortable marathon pace, which is probably going to be somewhere around ten minute miles. I started Bath well hydrated and fuelled, had two energy gels on the way round, one at about four miles and one at nine miles, and used three of the drink stations, so I'm happy that I can manage that side of things sensibly. Physically I felt great, none of the niggles I've experienced along the way have proved to be anything more serious and I didn't even have a blister to show for my supreme effort. My recovery was also good, I didn't experience any of the almost immediate stiffening up that I have in the past and my aches were minimal. So things are looking good for London, provided I make it through the final seven weeks of training intact.

Aside from the running, it was a great day in Bath all round. Myself and three of my children had breakfast at Clare's flat in Bristol before setting off for Bath. Clare had made delicious kedgeree, good running fuel as it turns out. Well Clare and I enjoyed it anyway; the children opted for toast and doughnuts, their tastes not yet having undergone the process of refinement. Thusly fed and watered, we drove over to my dad's house on the outskirts of Bath and he then dropped Clare and I down to the race village in the centre to do all our pre-race necessities - going to the toilet, pinning on our race numbers, attaching race chips, putting bags into storage, going to the toilet again, etc. The children came to watch the race later with their grandparents, uncle and cousins, they saw me run past on both laps and Keziah managed a grand total of 111 high-fives with runners (that was a few less than last year apparently). They love seeing all the runners in fancy dress and this year Sam said he found it inspiring to see people of all ages running the distance (which I interpret as code for, 'Wow, even old people can run'). The only person/character he saw drop out was Bugs Bunny. The day itself was seriously c..c..c..cold. It felt fine when we were running, but I was absolutely freezing before and after. I'm glad that I had a big woolly jumper and gloves in my bag to put on afterwards as well as my dress-sized Bath-half finisher's T shirt, otherwise I would have had to go to Pizza Express with Clare for our post-race celebratory food and alcoholic beverage in my foil blanket. Actually Clare did go in her foil blanket.

I love the post-race afterglow, the satisfaction of basking in the results of some serious effort. It actually has a lot in common with the feeling one has after giving birth. It goes something like, 'That was really hard, I'm so glad it's over, but look at my gorgeous baby/amazingly fast time/shiny medal (delete as applicable), it was all worthwhile for this!' In both scenarios it is also very satisfying to send out a massive amount of blowing one's own trumpet style texts and enjoy all the pat on the back replies as they come in one by one. And of course, to cap the day off nicely, there has to be a hot bubble bath.

Whilst my marathon training progresses well, the reverse could be said for the state of my house. Keeping on top of the housework is an ongoing challenge not made any easier by currently devoting anything up to ten hours a week to running. I'm including in that total the time it takes to get ready to go out and to shower afterwards. Superficial tidiness in some areas - ok, maybe only in one key area - can just about be maintained; meanwhile all around the dust is coming along nicely. I could perhaps use it to stuff something before too long. Piles of things to sort are multiplying and the potential to be surprised by something sticky, mucky or chaotic is increasing day-by-day. I keep telling myself that once the marathon is run I can get on top of things, although to be honest pre-marathon it wasn't that much better. Ok, to be more realistic, once the children have left home I might manage a clean and tidy house.

18 and 21 Mile Runs in the Bag

I did an eighteen-mile long run the weekend after Bath half-marathon. Being in the thick of marathon training and a sensible post-race recovery period don't seem mutually compatible, but fortunately I didn't seem to suffer any ill-effects for plunging straight back into the schedule with barely a pause for breath. The following weekend I ran my longest long run of twenty-one miles.

I now have the satisfaction of being able to say that there are only two more long runs to go on my training schedule before I start to taper towards race day. The *only* in that last sentence sounds a little blasé given that I still have many hard training miles to run, but it signifies that I do have a solid sense of having run through the scariest places on my training schedule and emerged on the other side in one piece. I can see the light at the end of the tunnel.

I use the words scary and running together intentionally, because running can be really scary sometimes. Maybe that seems a strange thing to say. Surely one could stop at any time during a run, even a race, without much more consequence than the inconvenience of a walk home or back to the start line (admittedly that could be a very long walk). And surely if a goal is too ambitious in practice, well just let it go and deal with the slight dent in your pride. It's not like being stuck on the side of Mount Everest in a blizzard, that's the definition of scary. I think, speaking for myself anyway, the fear comes when you want to achieve something, maybe have a new running or race distance in view or a time you want to achieve, but you worry that your ambition (which you may have broadcast very publicly) will take you to a place that your body and mind are not equipped for and you will end up a quivering, broken, humiliated wreck on the pavement. Interestingly though, I think the last few weeks have shown me that my body is actually capable of far more than I ever imagined if I treat it with respect and train wisely. It does seem that once you get to a certain level of fitness it is possible, with sensible pacing, hydration and nutrition, to run and just keep on running. I may experience points during a long run when I start to feel really fatigued, but often that feeling passes and five or ten minutes later I'm back into relatively comfortable running. I can see now how it's possible to run beyond 26.2 miles into ultra marathon territory (not that I have any designs on going there myself).

The eighteen-mile run was done straight through as all the traffic light crossings were showing in our favour as pedestrians. Often I run up to a traffic light crossing willing the little red man to be glowing brightly so I can take a breather even for fifteen seconds, but on that day all the little green men were out strutting their stuff. I tired noticeably after about fifteen miles and Graham took pity on me and amended the last bit of the route to avoid the final big hill. Our run time was 2:56 making an average of 9:47 minute miles, which I think is pretty respectable especially only a week after going flat-out for that PB in Bath (my middle-aged not very 'talented' version of flat-out anyway).

The following weekend we aimed for a long run of twenty miles but overshot a little, by a mile for myself and three for Graham who later got a telling off from his other running buddy, super-fast Nick - aka The Beast after his storming marathon debut at Dartmoor Vale last autumn - for doing such a long long run only three weeks out from his marathon. It was a hard run as we were both feeling tired but a fantastic route, which made it more enjoyable together with the huge sense of achievement afterwards. We started out from our usual point but then ventured well beyond familiar north Bristol running territory and through some of Bristol's most famous beauty spots including (with apologies to non-Bristolians as this may not mean much to you) The Downs, Clifton Suspension Bridge, Ashton Court and Avon Gorge. We stopped a couple of times for a few minutes to confer on the next bit of our route and to have a chug of water or down an energy gel, but otherwise we ran straight through, myself doing twenty one miles in 3:36 making my average pace 10:19 minute miles. I would get a slap on the wrist by the writers of The Non-Runner's Marathon Trainer if I were to use that time to conjecture a possible finishing time for my marathon, but of course I have fleetingly and I would be very happy with it. I'd say, based on my long runs so far, that my sensible marathon pace will be between 9:45 and 10:15 minute miles. It will be tempting to start out faster if I'm feeling fresh, which I should be after the training tapers down in the last three weeks, so I will have to keep an eye on my Garmin and slow down if necessary so I don't crash and burn in the second half. I really don't want to hit the wall if that can be avoided. That would be scary running. I am very pleased that I am injury free and certainly twenty-one miles is a long enough run for any underlying issues to show themselves. My main concern now is to get myself some new trainers and get them worn in as I have experienced some discomfort under the base of the second and third toes of my left foot during long runs recently, which could be down to worn out cushioning on the pair that I've been running in for over a year now. The new pair of trainers I bought over Christmas haven't had very much use yet as I had a wobble in confidence over whether they were substantial enough to use for my long runs.

I have been excited to feel recently and since surprising myself with how well I ran Bath half-marathon, that my running power is definitely coming from my core now (a legacy of years of ballet training is being very body-aware). This confirms for me the wisdom in the opinion of Danny Dreyer, author and pioneer of ChiRunning, that running with good form is the best strength training for running and that supplemental training (or cross-training) is not essential for building a strong core. Good, because I really don't have time for that. It is also confirmation that I have been able to successfully apply some of the ChiRunning techniques all on my own. A running coach who was manning a stall at my running club's AGM recently told me that you couldn't learn good running technique from a book. Well I beg to differ. Personally, I highly recommend the book and the ChiRunning technique, having been able to use it to transform my running style. I'm sure there are lots of other great resources, teachers and courses out there, but this is the one that came my way and I am very grateful that it did otherwise I'd still be running in the way Alexandra Heminsley describes in her book 'Running Like a Girl'.

> 'When I began running I tried very, very hard to do two things in order to show as much willing as possible: to bounce up and down as springily as possible, and to reach out as far as possible as I could with my heels. I interpreted both of these actions as indicators of serious commitment to my sport and a huge signifier of great athleticism. I could not have been more wrong.'

So, with eighteen and twenty one mile runs in the bag I am feeling much more confident, knowing I am within a whisker of the full marathon distance. Yes, admittedly that would be quite a long whisker, the kind of whisker my kids might read about in The Guinness Book of World Records alongside the grotesque pictures of long curly fingernails (big cringe and involuntary body shudder). My other weekly runs are generally two five miles and a midweek eight at the moment. Midweek runs often feel tougher than, or certainly as tough as, the long weekend runs. I feel like I am just getting through them dutifully so I can tick the boxes and they feel like hard work. I'm not sure why the shorter runs should feel that way aside from fatigue from the long run at the weekend, but maybe one factor could be having a more casual attitude to things like nutrition. For example, I would often go out to run in the morning midweek without anything more than a cup of tea inside me, but I probably ought to be eating something too, even for the five-mile runs. I often can't face food in the morning before running though, the thought of chewing my way through something when my appetite hasn't yet woken up really doesn't appeal. However, I have recently discovered that I can manage a small bowl of Ready Brek as there no chewing involved and it's suitably bland plus it's ideal nutritionally before running being high in carbohydrate.

I have a variety of running related reading on the go at the moment. Having discovered that's it's cheaper (and I guess more environmentally friendly) than a paper copy; I now download Women's Running onto my iPad. I normally read it cover to cover within a couple of days so I have been tempted to download other running magazines too, but so far I have resisted as it would become an expensive habit. I am also re-reading The Non-Runner's Marathon Trainer in step with my own training, as there is a chapter to go with each week of the programme. The other book I have on the go is one I downloaded onto my iPad for a few pounds called 'Running Shoes are a Girl's Best Friend' by Margreet Deitz, which is a collection of interviews with ladies who run. I am persevering with it but finding it a little dry and serious with the notable exception of one lady who with complete honesty admitted that she only runs so she can eat whatever she likes without putting on weight and what she does eat is generally complete junk. Hats off to you madam for being so frank. Maybe the lady in question is not a running role model, but I did appreciate the absence of pretense. Perhaps the way that the questions were put to the interviewees only gave a limited scope for exploring their lives and their interest in running, but so far I've found that I'm not itching to read more about any of the women whereas normally when I read other people's stories my human curiosity is engaged and I feel like I would love to know more. However the interviews did bring out some themes that I identified with and found interesting, one of those being that a lot of women would place the weight loss and toning effects of running high on their list of reasons why they do it which I would echo myself. Running is a great way of kick-starting a broader lifestyle overhaul. Once you've been training for long enough to feel stronger and more toned in a way that you probably haven't since you were a lot younger, or maybe never have, it becomes obvious that if you start eating more sensibly too you have got to be onto a winning combination. Put it this way, there is considerably less of me since I figured this out.

One of the other themes that I noticed is that as a result of the many benefits that running brings, it can become something that people become super-obsessional about. The language that some people use when talking running is suggestive of an addiction. Running has become a necessity without which the person feels their life would be incomplete, maybe even unlivable, and of course that can't help but make me think of Mark. Personally I hope someone will be brave enough to slap me a few times round the face if I start to get that way about my running, it is great to feel fit and enjoy the challenges and rewards of running but I wouldn't choose for my satisfaction with and fulfillment in life to hinge on that alone. I think that I can understand how running comes to mean so much to some people though. As much as some may plead themselves to be an exception to this rule, I do subscribe to the theory that we as humans are hardwired to look for security in and give devotion to something. If we don't worship a deity, we will, consciously or otherwise, always find something else to worship and build our lives around. We might be devoted to ourselves, another person, a belief system, a pet, a lifestyle, a hobby, a desirable emotional state, ambition, money, or a combination of the above. Looked at in that light getting hooked on running does make sense, but I just struggle to understand why someone would knowingly choose to place all, or at least lot of, their eggs in such a temporal basket as running, there are too many cracks in the pavement out there - take that in a literal or metaphorical sense - just waiting to trip you up, smash your eggs and end your running days. Maybe I'm trying to ascribe too much conscious rationality to the devotional life. I guess it runs in a deeper and more mysterious vein sometimes.

Either the confession about the state of my house, having a bit of extra time or a combination of both, have spurred me to some feats of cleaning and sorting over the last few weeks and it's encouraging to be reminded that actually the mess is always worse in my head. In other words, when I get stuck in it never takes as long to get things in order as I worried it would. In a few weeks time I may be able to say I've run a marathon, I have a clean house and I am still just an ordinary woman. There's certainly nothing wonderful about the way I manage my life as my husband will verify, it's all fairly haphazard. All of which just to goes show that if I can do it anyone can.

Journal Entry 23 – 28th March 2013

Arriving at the Taper

Wow! I looked at my sticker covered training plan in the kitchen the other day and was suddenly struck by the realisation that I have completed the hardest section of the plan and it feels like that time has just flown by. It's as if someone pressed the fast-forward button. Now I'm heading into the post-marathon taper period. Amazing! I had anticipated some hard weeks with the mental effort and discipline required to complete the long runs being every bit as taxing as the physical side, but being able to do those runs with a friend and someone who, as it turns out, is a good running match in terms of pace, goals, etc. and not on my own as I had initially anticipated, has made a huge difference. What a blessing. It feels fantastic to have stayed free of injury and to be at this point already feeling strong, confident and excited. I say already because although the training obviously hasn't taken any less time than the plan always dictated it would, the companionship has given me wings. Without it the experience would have been closer to ground level. Think wading through treacle. Some people love to run alone, not I.

Last week my registration letter and information magazine for the marathon arrived. Exciting. I have to take the letter with some ID to the marathon expo in London on one of the days running up to the event to get my race number and kit bag. My plan is to go to the expo on the Friday when I arrive in London so that I can avoid the crowds on Saturday and keep that as a quiet restful day before running on Sunday. Clare has offered to wait on me hand and foot on Saturday so that I hardly need to move. I'm not sure if I've ever had that offered before, even after giving birth. What a quality friend. The magazine has all the bits of information runners and their spectators need to know about where to be when and how to get there. There is free travel on race day for marathon runners on much of London Transport, which is a bonus. Also I see, and this appeals to me as a true Brit who can chain-drink tea, there is a tea and coffee station in the pre-race area although, on further reflection, at that stage I should probably be thinking about emptying my bladder not re-filling it. I will be in the blue start area, which is in Blackheath, somewhere I haven't been since I lodged there for a short while when I was a student at The Laban Institute for Movement and Dance in New Cross after leaving school.

London has fond associations for me as my parents are from Edmonton and Enfield in north London, so I visited lots as a child to stay with my grandparents. My favourite childhood memories of London are riding the Underground - I still love it - and visiting places like Covent Garden and Harrods with my mum. And then there are lots of memories attached to my mum's mum Louisa's house, a little terraced house in Edmonton over the road from the shopping centre. I can remember so much about the house, all sorts of details that would probably seem far less fascinating as an adult. The wallpapers, the Lino in the kitchen with its join in the middle of the room that had been made with thick tape, the magnetic soap-holder in the bath-room, the seat on the outside loo that used to sit slightly shy of the porcelain so that when you sat down on it it might pinch a good chunk of flesh in between the two - ouch, I was more careful after that one time - the 1950s crockery (probably highly collectible now), the fascination (coming from a non-smoking household) with my Granddad's ashtrays and the contents thereof (and how dismayed I was when I made him an ashtray in pottery at primary school then watched him actually stub a cigarette out in it spoiling its pristine appearance forever). I could go on and on, but to share one last special memory, when we had toast at this Nanny's house we would make it by putting a slice of bread on a toasting fork and toasting it in front of the gas fire. Not only was this process highly novel and exciting but the toast itself always tasted special too being spread with butter - we had to endure 'healthier' margarine at home - and lime marmalade and being made from a white bloomer loaf Nanny bought from the bakery in the shopping centre. The loaf always had fascinating little bobbles on the bottom from the tray it had been baked on. Such nostalgia.

So, back to running, last week I ordered some new trainers through Amazon, some running socks (do runner's need special socks? My answer would be yes if you want to avoid blisters) and a gel belt (not a belt made of gel but a belt to hold energy gels). I have run in the trainers all this week and am very happy with them although disappointingly they haven't cured the under-toe discomfort, so I think that must be down to the amount of miles I've been running and/or the toe I broke last year, not to running in old trainers after all. I'm never quite sure what to do with the trainers that become the old pair once the new pair is acquired, sometimes they're still in good enough condition to take to a charity shop but I'm never sure if I should do that knowing that I've already run the best miles that they had in them. Suggestions on a postcard please, because I have around 4 pairs that need re-homing.

Having completed my final long run - eighteen miles with only a two minute time difference from the last time I ran that distance; a pretty consistent pace seems to have emerged - I now find myself in a strange place with slightly limbo-like qualities. I've done the hard training work and now there is what feels like a big chunk of time with significantly reduced training before marathon day. All the marathon training plans I've looked at have a taper period in the last few weeks before the race with training mileage being cut down significantly to allow for rest and recovery. Apparently it is normal during this stage to feel anxious that one is not doing enough to stay in peak condition and that fitness could drop off. Normal but unfounded. Muscles benefit from time to heal from all the rigours they've been put through and enough training is still happening to maintain fitness. Interestingly, although the 'enough' makes the training during the taper sound rather second-rate, the mileage involved remains very respectable for a week's worth of running - twenty seven miles on the first taper week of three, nineteen on the second - which just goes to show how one's judgement of what qualifies as a lot of miles changes during the course of marathon training. I find myself coming out with statements like, 'I'm only doing nine miles today'. Since when did a nine-mile run warrant the prefix only? Since some time during February I think. I am experiencing some anxiety about the reduced mileage, but the bigger issue seems to be that I've kind of gone off the idea of training runs full stop. I am and I will do them conscientiously, but they're starting to feel more and more of a chore now. I do find that getting my running gear on helps me to get into the zone and then it's just a case of getting on with it so that I can sticker my chart.

I think what would be of benefit now is taking time to refocus on what started me on this marathon journey and all that the big day means beyond my own achievement. But that will have to wait for another day. 12.30 has me feeling ready for bed, not for deep and meaningful reflections. Hmmm, those earlier nights haven't generally happened.

Journal Entry 24 – 2nd April 2013

Nearly There: A Time to Reflect

Easter finds my family back visiting with Pete's folk in Lincolnshire. Three months have not seen many degrees difference in temperature up here thanks to this endless winter we seem to be having. This time though I am running in the dry, there are no puddles to skirt around on the country roads I run along and no rain to contend with. Plenty of wind though. It's good to have a change from running largely - although not exclusively, since teaming up with route-master extraordinaire Graham - around the pavements of suburbia. On my run yesterday and had I been less pre-occupied with the act of running, I could have stroked two very friendly looking horses, helped myself to free manure, bought either some farm eggs or a baby guinea pig for £8.00, or taken up the invitation on a poster to attend an unspecified 'social event' at the village church at 7.30 p.m.

So now that the end goal of this training in all weathers and various locations heaves into view, have I been good and stuck to my chosen training plan? By and large that's a solid yes. I have skipped two five-mile runs to give myself extra recovery time and gone just a little off-piste with the longer runs, but otherwise, yes. Twelve, fourteen, three times sixteen and two times eighteen-mile long runs instead became a 13.67 (I was too tired to round up to a tidy fourteen that day if you remember), 16, 13.3 (Bath Half-marathon as measured by my Garmin), 18, 21, 16 and 18. Now I tot it up, the total mileage for those runs hasn't been much different to the original plan (I've only run an extra six miles), it's just that I upped the mileage a little earlier than recommended, fortunately without ill-effect. I have read in several places that it's unwise to increase mileage by more than 10% from one week to the next or to increase the distance of a particular type of run by more than 10% at a time and I may possibly have broken that rule of thumb but not too drastically. As far as being a truly diligent athlete goes, I will admit that my pre-run warm-ups and post-run stretches have gone down the pan recently. I confess that I don't tend to bother with them anymore. To begin with this wasn't a deliberate decision, I guess intuitively it just didn't seem like either was making enough difference for me to ensure that I made time for it. Up until now I have done the pre-run warm-ups from the ChiRunning book (not stretches, but rather mobilising and opening up the joints) and three or four different stretches after running. To go some way towards excusing my slackness, I am on my feet most of the day being fairly active even if that's just around the home, so I suppose I am rarely, if ever, springing up to run from an inactive state in terms of needing to warm-up. As far as the post-run stretching goes, it just doesn't feel like it makes any tangible difference because my recovery has been consistently good for months with or without it and I am more concerned that I could stretch carelessly and do myself a mischief of some kind. Needless to say, don't follow my example, being contrary as it is to all the usual advice. Although I did read an article about stretching in Women's Running magazine this month that suggested that stretching was more critical for runners with a fairly sedentary lifestyle - i.e. sitting on their arses for large portions of the day - which certainly isn't me. I would say that most days I don't spend any significant amount of time sitting down until about

10.00pm when Pete and I might watch something on iPlayer before going to bed.

I have totalled up my training mileage and it works out at just over four hundred miles so far for the marathon training programme and just over five hundred if I include the base fitness training I started at the end of September after having time out of running with my broken toe. That's a lot less than a more advanced runner might undertake for a marathon, but it seems to have been enough to build my fitness and confidence for distance running and the 21st of April will show whether it stands me in good stead for the 26.2 miles. Eek, only ten days to go now! Writing that sentence (on the 11th of April, I take a while to finish my entries sometimes) just gave me butterflies in my tummy. I included my total training mileage on a Facebook status update this week in an attempt to muster up some more donations for Place2Be, but it doesn't seem to have had the desired effect. Without overlooking the amazing donations made already - thank you everybody - which have made a good inroad towards my target of £1000, I do get the sense that there is more giving fatigue around than I had initially anticipated. Admittedly I could do more to inspire people (maybe I should be organising cake sales or tea parties?) but I just don't have the leftover time or energy required. The slow trickle of donations this time, and indeed my other fundraising experiences since I started running, have made me more sympathetic to other's fundraising efforts and more likely to donate myself because I understand how hard it can be to generate support. Let's face it, we all find it a lot easier to spend £5 or £10 on coffee and cake than to give the same amount to charity. So another round of emails are on the to do list, although I'll have to try a different angle to last time as that didn't generate any donations at all. Bah.

Now that the event is nearly upon me, I have been thinking again about why I am running this marathon. What deep meaning and significance is there behind it, if any? I have come to the conclusion that actually it's really quite simple. I am running Mark's marathon for him. I'm running the marathon he worked so hard for but didn't get to experience himself. Would he have appreciated my actions? To be quite frank, not necessarily, neither the sentiment nor my comparatively snail-like efforts (this is someone who ran a 10k in 44:45 when he'd only been running for five or six months and didn't have a history of being super-fit). I think I have to be honest and admit that perhaps this is more about me, about me finding a way to hold on to a small part of Mark for a little bit longer because otherwise it would just be too easy to forget him. Sadly our experience as siblings shows how easy it is for brothers and sisters to grow up alongside each other yet have no depth to their relationship so that as adults and having moved out of the confines of the family home, there seems no reason for their lives to remain connected. To fill in some history, Mark's mother died before his first birthday leaving his father, John, with two young sons. My parents divorced when I was around three years old so that my mother, Lyn, was left on her own with my baby brother and myself. John and Lyn's worlds collided shortly afterwards and a union of families ensued. So I grew up for the majority of my childhood with my brother, Dave, and stepbrothers Paul and Mark. In age we were all within three years of each other and Paul and I, being only two months apart, were in the same year at school (which caused some confusion because of our different looks and surnames, apparently some people spent years thinking we were going out with each other). As children, Mark and I largely ignored each other and it wasn't until we were both in our twenties that we chose to spend any time together. I'm not even sure how it first came about now, but over a few years we occasionally socialised together and it pleased me a lot to feel that we were finally getting to know each other and enjoying each others company. Then somehow our fragile relationship fell apart again. I entered into the world of making babies, marriage and growing a family of my own and despite my attempts over the ensuing twelve year period, Mark just didn't engage with me ever again. After my own wedding and while Mark was still in Bristol before his move to Oxford, I saw him at Dave's wedding, bumped into him once on the doorstep of the family home, once in a local supermarket and that was it. I wrote letters regularly to keep him up to speed with the family news over the years he spent in Oxford but I never received a reply and when he moved to Leeds I only knew because the new occupant at his old address returned a letter to me. I tracked Mark down through good old Google, but found it progressively harder to keep on writing to a faceless university email address and my attempts became fewer and further apart. I never knew why Mark disengaged from me and wondered about it often, sometimes to myself, sometimes out loud in my letters to him, but that will now remain a mystery. So I guess I've just written round in a circle, back to what it means to me to be running Mark's marathon. This is about me making a statement that through all those years when, for whatever reason, it was too difficult for Mark to be in touch, I still thought of him and wanted to connect. Perhaps if he'd known in his last few years that I was a fellow runner, that might have sparked a response, I guess now it's like I'm saying, "Hey! We do have something in common, we both run. I get what you were into. I understand what it meant to you". The thing is, I'm not sure who I'm making that statement to other than myself, because Mark's not around now to hear it. Will the 21st of April be an emotional day for me? I know some people are assuming that it will be because of the story behind it. I honestly don't know. I'm not anticipating feeling that way as I'm not a very emotional person, this is just something I wanted to do, but I'll let you know in due course.

Journal entry 25 – 15th April 2013

Marathon Week is Here!

Only 6 days to go until marathon day! I really feel like someone pressed the fast forward button now.

The taper has been an up and down experience with the ups where I would have expected the downs to be and vice versa. The first of the three taper weeks, where the mileage hadn't decreased too drastically apart from on the long run day (down to a mere ten miles), I was feeling really quite anxious about maintaining fitness and I had to keep telling myself that I could trust the experts to know what they are talking about. Conversely, now that I'm down to virtually nothing (I have three and four mile runs left this week plus maybe a two mile run on Friday once in London), I'm feeling very relaxed about it all. Go figure. I'm alternating between nerves and excitement when I think about the big day, but so far excitement has the edge. This is the time to think positively, trust that I've given the training my utmost and that I've done all I can to be ready - after all if I haven't, it's too late to do anything else now.

Graham ran his first marathon in Taunton on the 7th April in a time of 4:10. Brilliant. It went really well for him so it's encouraging for me to hear firsthand that even a first-timer can run a marathon confidently. Realistically I will be quite a way off that kind of time as Graham is a faster runner - he has completed a half-marathon in 1:47 compared to my best of 2:01 - but it helps me to get a ball-park idea of how long it might take. Yes, I know I'm not supposed to be doing that. The advice from the horse's mouth is to stick to my pre-decided marathon pace no matter what people around me are doing and to drink little and often on the way round. Graham's marathon meant a lot to him personally as it was the fruit of a turning point in his life a few years back when he realised he needed to lose weight - five stone - and get back his health and fitness. Onwards and upwards. He's already planning his next marathon. I'd better watch out, he'll have me signed up for another one too if I'm not careful. Graham's friend Nick finished Taunton - his second marathon - in the ludicrously fast time of 3:04 giving him automatic entry to London Marathon next year because he's officially super-fast for an old fart. Apologies for being so irreverent Nick, I believe the correct terminology is 'veteran' or 'good for age' or some such pseudo-polite terminology. I ran with Nick recently and it was good. Admittedly it felt like I was running quite fast while he was on a very slow recovery run, but that's ok.

Points of interest from recent runs include, the reappearance of rain after a good three months absence from the scene (fortunately only gentle rain, we are being reacquainted gradually), an unplanned foray into the local countryside, and the reappearance of a friendly face.

Where we live is on the outskirts of Bristol so very close to proper countryside, but being a city girl who grew up near the city centre, I don't naturally think to explore what we have almost on our doorstep unless someone else takes us out for a ramble. So I'm rather proud that whilst doing a five mile run a few days ago (and having drastically overestimated the distance involved in running through the small local town of Thornbury where Keziah's swimming club meets twice a week), I found myself, in pursuit of adequate mileage, running along narrow country roads liberally coated in manure and without any pavement. Dun dun daah (that being a dramatic sound effect). Favourite moments from that uncharacteristically adventurous run were the little Baptist church that looked very much alive and cared for and very much not abandoned then turned into a quirky home, and seeing a signpost to somewhere delightfully named Duckhole. I didn't follow it to find out if there was a hole full of ducks somewhere.

And the friendly face? That belonged to Carrie, who I mentioned having met on a Sole Sisters run months ago but who had then disappeared from the scene. She's been busy getting married and studying so I guess those are good enough excuses for taking a bit of time out. It was great to be able to tell Carrie that I was running the London marathon imminently as she has run it herself and the last time we spoke I was still only hatching the idea. Hilariously she told me that when she ran she was dressed as a ladybird but a friend complained that she didn't manage to spot her (no pun intended) on the way round and it transpired that in a moment of absentmindedness Carrie had mistakenly said she would be dressed as a bumble bee. In terms of identifying a runner by their fancy dress, you don't want to be muddling up a Superman with a Batman when there are thousands of runners to look through, or, in the case of Bath half-marathon favourite costumes, confusing a boob with some other enlarged, air-filled fancy dress body part. I am absolutely in awe of anyone who can run in fancy dress particularly the more cumbersome costumes. Those inflatable boobs - which I have seen worn on fronts and backs - sway from side to side quite violently not unlike the real thing if unconstrained by a sports bra and they squeak too. I was nearly knocked sideways by an enormous nipple in Bath whilst trying to overtake. Forget fancy dress, I don't even like to run with a water bottle in my hand. So next time you see someone bravely running in any kind of special get-up, be sure to give him or her an extra loud cheer. My kids will love looking out for all the weird and wonderful fancy dress in London and I look forward to comparing notes with them afterwards.

This week is set to become a week full of lists. I have three are on the go already. Things to take to London, things the kids need to pack for London, and assorted other things to organise for and around the trip. But forget the lists, they're essential but boring. More than that, this is turning out to be a week of excitement. It's unexpected but massively welcome. I had anticipated feeling racked with nerves at this point but I'm not, that was last week. I am genuinely really excited about the whole weekend, even the actual act of running for 26.2 miles. That being said, I am maintaining my respect for the distance and I know that I must abide by all the golden rules: Pacing, hydration & nutrition during the run and lots of carbs and adequate sleep over the days before. I hope that is all of the golden rules, because I can't think of any more.

My last pre-marathon run with Sole Sisters was great in all respects - great running and great conversation. I got to talk to the amazing Mary. Amazing because she is also running the London marathon (her first too), she has two young children and she works full-time as a school headmistress. Could this be the real life Wonder woman? In her spare time (spare time? Ok, maybe when other people think she's just nipped to the loo), does she don star-spangled pants and fly off to beat up baddies? Quite possibly. Mary and I have both been running with Sole Sisters for a while but this was the first time we'd had a proper chat. We plan to meet up at the blue start on Sunday for some pre-marathon solidarity and Mary will be hoping that her current injury allows her to get round (a foot tendon thing). Frustratingly another runner from the club, Karen, hoping to run her second London marathon also has an injury (a torn calf muscle) and was unsure on Monday whether she would be able to attempt the run at all. She said she had shed many tears at the prospect of not being able to. Needless to say I am counting myself very blessed to be at the end of my training injury-free. Thankfully all of the niggles I have experienced along the way have been just that. London here I come!

Journal Entry 26 – 19th April 2013

On the Train to London

I am writing this on the train to London.

The elderly lady sitting next to me said a polite hello then fell asleep almost immediately. We managed to exchange a couple of brief polite sentences about the weather then she was asleep as quickly as turning off a light. I fully expect that her head will come to rest on my shoulder soon because she is doing the thing where you tip over sideways as you fall asleep then wake up with a start when you loll over too far. It's quite impressive really, no sooner has the falling sensation woken the poor lady up than she has - quite literally - nodded straight off again. She obviously wants to sleep and doesn't appear to be trying desperately to stay awake so perhaps I should just offer her my shoulder as a head-rest now and have done with it?

So, departure day has arrived. The lists have been worked through, goodbyes until marathon day have been said in words, kisses and hugs, my friend Sara has dropped me at the train station whilst whisking Keziah off for a morning at Bristol Museum with her kids, and I am now on the 10:01 train from Bristol Parkway to London Paddington hoping that I have indeed packed everything I need in my backpack that is as heavy as a breeze-block. Making your luggage compact does not necessarily equal travelling light it would seem. I know I have definitely got my trainers, registration letter and ID for the expo to pick up my race number, so I can run on Sunday if nothing else. Or indeed run in nothing else if necessary, but that's not a good mental image. I have just enjoyed a delicious and entirely guilt-free Pain au Chocolat with my takeaway cup of Earl Grey tea - it is called carb-loading and is an important part of my pre-race preparation, there are some perks that come with marathon training. In fact I have two more things that also fit into that category from the last week. A few days ago another amazing Mary - I know a few of them - presented me at our home education co-op day with a 'good luck running the marathon' chocolate cake complete with a rendition of myself in icing. And another friend, Petra, has booked me a post-marathon sports massage. What great friends I have been blessed with. To give me a further boost, my fundraising for Place2Be has risen to over 60% of my target amount this week.

Sleeping Beauty miraculously managed to wake up at just the right time to get off the train at Didcot Parkway. Her place has been taken by someone who is very wide awake and reading the paper.

I know this is a high-speed train, but the journey really is going a little too fast. I feel like I need more time to mentally adjust from home and the bustle of kids to London with all that the weekend holds. Sitting in a backwards-facing seat isn't helping either, it seems to increase the sense of speed as the countryside whizzes past the window. All those months of preparation and now I will transition into the event weekend that this has been heading towards with a journey of less than two hours.

I have been hydrating like mad for the last twenty-four hours, which of course then equals weeing like mad. So annoyingly I may have to wriggle out of my window seat in a minute and find the on-board loo. Or then again maybe I'll wait until we're nearer to Paddington so I don't need to go again as soon as I get there because if I do I'll have to pay for the privilege. As far back as I can remember, travelling up to London with my mum, they have always charged for use of the toilets at Paddington station. It just doesn't seem right somehow to have to pay to pee.

The sun is out today giving us glorious blue skies. It's still chilly though. The weather forecast for Sunday is looking good. Spring has finally decided to arrive and recently I have been able to run in just one or two layers. On Monday I ran in only a T-shirt, it has been a long while since I could do that (well, not literally in only a T shirt, that would be weird). Tuesday morning brought the awful news about the bombings at the Boston marathon with three dead and many injured, some very seriously. The organisers of the London marathon have been quick to offer reassurance that the event will go ahead and that they are confident in their security arrangements. There will be a thirty second silence before the elite runners start as a mark of respect and all runners will receive a black ribbon to wear.

My plans for this my first day of four in London involve meeting up with a friend from my youth recently rediscovered through Facebook, Michael, who I haven't seen for twenty three years (now that makes me feel old), going to the expo to register, trying to find Sam an extra surprise present for his thirteenth birthday on Monday (he's spending that day with me in London) and meeting Clare from her coach at Victoria. Oh, and of course lots more eating and drinking to fuel for marathon day, no alcohol though. My plan for tomorrow is to conserve energy for race day by doing as little as possible apart from further eating and drinking.

"Ladies and gentlemen, the train has now arrived at London Paddington". This is it. Let marathon weekend commence!

Journal Entry 27 – 20th April 2013

Race Day is Tomorrow

As I start to write today at somewhere around midday, the pattern of my morning has looked something like this - Eat, drink, tussle with my nerves, take deep breaths, go for a wee, repeat. This morning all of a sudden I am so nervous. I feel as if I've been hit with a laboratory-prepared concentrated dose of nerves straight into a vein. A jittery tummy is making eating a challenge and my appetite seems to have gone absent without leave, I'm having to resort to a grazing approach to eating, slow and steady. It's hard to eat enough when I'm feeling like this, but I know that I need to fuel well today so that I'm fully loaded with energy supplies for tomorrow. Before I write any more about the day before the big day, let me return to yesterday.

On arriving at Paddington station I was met by a smiling Michael on the platform. Very little has changed over the course of twenty-three years either in appearance or friendship apart from something of a lack of hair on Michael's side (winking emoji). The years have been mutually kind to us. Over a brilliantly busy afternoon, with Michael for company, I did all the things I needed to in order to be ready for Sunday and to make sure I could have downtime today. We dived into the marathon expo at five minutes before closing time after an, "Excel Centre please Guv and step on the gas!" black cab ride. You have to do a few things in your lifetime that make you feel like you're in a movie. The expo was pretty much empty of punters as it was late in the day, so I was able to go straight to the collection points for my race number, official kit bag (for baggage storage during the marathon) and timing chip. The people manning the stalls in the hall who were representing the main charities or selling running-related merchandise, were standing around looking mentally off-duty and obviously counting down the minutes until home time, so we didn't have a good look around. Visiting the expo was a bit of a non-event, but at least it was easy to do the registration essentials without queuing or battling through crowds as I may have had to if I'd left it until the next day and I didn't have the opportunity to be tempted to spend money that I probably shouldn't. I did buy a headband, which suddenly seemed a useful extra bit of kit for the marathon after an annoying run the other day when my hair kept blowing forward and sticking to the sweat on my face. I also got my pre-race goody bag and some freebies for the kids. Then it was time for another 'Don't spare the horses!' dash across central London (this time on the Underground) to meet Clare off her coach at Victoria.

Returning to today. I didn't sleep as well as I hoped to last night in the very nice and definitely-more-up-market-than-a-Travelodge Hilton hotel room. I woke up ridiculously early this morning, dutifully drank a glass of water, tried and failed to get back to sleep, drank another glass of water, gave up on trying to sleep, got up and had a bath (whilst drinking a further glass of water), then, at a more civilised hour and once Clare had joined me in the land of the living, went out for a stroll around Canary Wharf to find a cafe to drink yet more water in. You can see the pattern I mentioned earlier emerging. Don't let the prolific hydration alarm you though, I didn't drink so much that I was in danger of hyponatraemia (water intoxication - potentially fatal) but I did drink a lot by my usual standards. I'm generally more up for a cup of tea at regular intervals rather than drinking eight glasses of water a day because it's good for me (or whatever it is that health advisors recommend). The reason for my copious water consumption is that I am hoping I will be well hydrated before race day so that I don't have to drink too much in the morning hence avoiding the need to go the loo ten times before the start (which is difficult when you've got to queue for ten minutes or more each time), nor will I have to start running with more in my bladder than I'm comfortable with after having given birth to four children if you know what I mean. Let's hope this strategy works, because if I get the bladder fullness/emptiness calculations wrong, my trusty back-up Tena pad will have to save the day. My apologies to the guys and girls on the other side of childbirth to me, I know you really didn't want to hear that. Too much information?

INTERLUDE...

I am now writing later in the day. It is the evening and Clare and I are having some writing time in the hotel bar. Clare is writing a vampire novel.

What a great day it has turned out to be enjoying the glorious sunshine under clear blue skies at various café-type establishments. As the day wore on the intense nerves thankfully mellowed and the excitement began to creep back in rising to a crescendo with a hilarious photo session with Clare in the hotel room when I did my pre-marathon kit check. Oh how we laughed. I wanted to try everything on and make sure I was happy with my choice of clothes to run in, that I knew where I could pin my race number whilst still leaving the Place2Be logo visible on my top and circumnavigating the gel belt, and just to get back into the running zone after a few days without donning Lycra or trainers at all. Clare, who has willingly taken on the role of official photographer, snapped Mobot (Andreabot) photos, fake running action shots, marathon convict holding race number, artistically arranged trainers next to race number, and more besides. Much fun and hilarity was had. I think I can say at the tail end of this day that thankfully the silliness and a growing excitement has kicked those nerves into touch. Phew.

Amongst the other things that proved strangely effective in calming my nerves, was Clare's hilarity at a few near-misfortunes that befell me during the afternoon. At one point I tripped up - bear in mind that this is the day before my much prepared for marathon - fortunately avoiding twisting, tearing, breaking or spraining finely trained marathon-ready body parts. But did Clare wait to laugh until after she had checked that I was ok? No, she guffawed the second that I stumbled, in fact she fairly howled with laughter. Clare then took further mirth at my accidentally pouring a large quantity of hot water from a dribbling teapot all over my mobile phone, aka essential marathon news updates communication device. I think some of my nervous tension must have transferred to her and she was experiencing that strange anomaly when laughter strikes at inappropriate moments like when we're surprised by an unexpected situation. Either that or she'd been secretly slipping something a bit stronger in her tea when I wasn't looking (probably when I was in the loo again). I will always remember being overcome with the giggles at secondary school when my form group was told the news that our teacher's son had died in a tragic accident. Of course it wasn't actually funny, but embarrassingly that came out as my nervous reaction on hearing such shocking news. On this considerably less serious occasion, with no ill effects from either mishap, I could laugh along too and be grateful to Clare for helping me to lighten up.

In terms of being race ready, I have managed to eat a good portion of my food in carbohydrate form today. I haven't eaten a lot overall - no huge bowls of pasta - but hopefully enough. The principal behind eating plenty of carbohydrates in the run up to race day is that by doing so you will be giving your body the correct fuel in sufficient quantity for it to create maximum stores of glycogen (a readily available energy source) in the muscles. There are normally sports drinks and/or gels (which contain simple carbohydrates) on the way round half or full marathons so that once your body's glycogen stores are depleted - or I guess ideally before that happens, which is apparently after only about 45 minutes of running - you can top-up on the go. The need for the appropriate muscle fuel to successfully run mile after mile explains the importance of having a race strategy planned out in advance. For example it is essential to think of the following: Will you take your own energy gels with you? When will you use them on the way round? When and what will you drink? - Sports drinks or water? Which drink stations will you use? - Some of them or all of them? I will be doing my final bit of homework and making a definite plan before bed tonight. The carb-loading low point of the day was an instant pot noodle type thing that I tried to make myself eat back in the hotel room to make up for not having much appetite earlier in the day. It was pretty grim and after Clare taste tested it for herself and pronounced it to be little better than slops, my noble attempts to get it down were abandoned - it was true, it didn't taste that great - and the rest of the noodles were flushed down the loo.

It has been great to have the day in London with all my training done to the best of my ability and time to relax and absorb that this is it, I'm here and as ready as I can be to run the marathon. It is so great that Mark allowed himself three nights around the marathon when he booked the hotel. I would probably have only given myself two in my planning but three feels like it will be perfect. It seems too much of a momentous occasion to be rushed into and out of. It has been exciting to see the London skyline - The Shard and London Eye are visible from my hotel room window - and the preparations being made for tomorrow. Clare and I walked past the eighteen-mile marker being erected just a short way up the road from the hotel and there are lots of temporary metal roadside barriers in place already. I didn't feel intimidated by seeing the eighteen-mile marker, which is encouraging.

Pete, mum and the children have all arrived in London and are safely installed in their hotel. I have been pretty ruthless about not travelling across London to see them today and they haven't felt adventurous enough to come and find me. I am a mum off-duty until this marathon is done; multi-tasking is on hold unless it involves running and drinking at the same time. I am taking a rare break from being the adult in charge but I will look forward to seeing everyone again on the way round the course tomorrow.

I've had encouragement and good luck wishes over the phone (mercifully undamaged by the water), so now, kit bag all packed, it is time to try and get some sleep (perchance to dream. Good dreams I hope though, not the I-need-to-run-but-my-legs-won't-move sort tonight please). Tomorrow is the day I have been training towards for nearly seven months. The alarm on my iPad is set to go off at 6.00 a.m. playing a track appropriately entitled 'We are running'. My thanks to Keziah for the iPad alarm setting tutorial before I left home. The mass race start is at 10.00 a.m. so that should give plenty of time to get up and get to where I need to be.

Journal Entry 28 – 21st April 2013

Running Mark's Marathon

I didn't need the 6.00 a.m. alarm, I was already awake a while before then. This was too auspicious a day it would seem for carefree slumbering. I wonder how many marathons it takes until the night before feels just like any other night? Again, answers on a postcard.

All kitted up, dutifully fuelled with a dose of pre-race Ready Brek and Clare packed up so she could head back to Bristol on the train with my family later after the marathon, we headed off for the blue start area at Blackheath, an easy journey on the Docklands Light Railway - which has become very familiar over these last few days - from South Quay, changing to an overground train for the last bit. We picked up more marathon runners at the stations along the journey and by the time we got to Blackheath at about 8.00 a.m. in glorious sunshine, there was a steady stream of Lycra clothed, red kit bag bedecked bodies heading out of the station and up the hill to the Heath. Being in good time and able to see that it was only a short walk to the runner's enclosure, we decided there was time for a coffee in Costa (water for me though). My nerves were under control after their freak out yesterday and I was feeling calm and ready for the marathon but I empathised - given how I'd felt the previous day

- with a female runner in the queue at the counter who appeared to be hyperventilating. She seemed to think a coffee would help but I'm not so sure that was the way to go myself, coffee normally has the reverse effect on me. I hope she was ok.

With the ease with which strangers talk to each other on momentous days like this, we struck up conversation with the other people sat on the high stools by the window and, in so doing, became acquainted with the Guinness World Record holder for knitting the longest scarf whilst running a marathon (hoping to beat her previous record today) and a 'fast for age' female runner a few years older than me who has only been running for a little longer than myself yet was hoping to achieve a time of around 3:30. I was sipping water very slowly at this point trying not to take on too much unnecessary fluid before the race, but toilets - even a couple of hours before the start - were clearly fast becoming much sought after and there was a long queue in the cafe already.

I exchanged some texts with fellow Sole Sister Mary around 8.30 a.m. She was already inside the runners' start area and we agreed that I'd call her once I was in too and we'd meet. Clare and I grabbed another runner to take a few final photos of us, said our goodbyes until later and she headed off to the seven mile point on the course hoping to catch a glimpse of Mo Farah and the elite runners.

By this point the steady trickle of runners heading across the Heath had grown to a constant flow with an air of calm anticipation. What a difference it makes when the sun is out, it was still chilly though and I was glad that I'd brought my running gloves, a jacket to discard at the start and an extra layer besides; I wouldn't have wanted to spend two hours shivering before we got running. With the sun so bright, I was also pleased that I'd remembered at the last minute to pack my running sunglasses (another Lidl bargain) and as it turned out I wore them all the way round. They are so light that you can't even feel that you've got them on. I hadn't thought to bring sunscreen for my nose and I knew it would be glowing brightly later in the day if the sun kept shining as it was. Who knew the weather would be so perfect that day? Not the weather forecasters, they'd predicted cloud cover.

Once inside the start area, I handed over my kit bag to go onto the lorry that would transport it to the finish and bravely took a pee in the female urinals. This is how a female urinal works, because you've got to be wondering: You pick up a cardboard contraption on the way into the urinal enclosure that, once in place, funnels your wee so that you can do it standing up like a bloke would. Ingenious. A couple of points are worth noting though. Firstly, the urinals are a little too high for short people like me; I had to stand on tiptoe to be able to point my cardboard downwards into it. Secondly, when removing the P-Mate (actual name), remember that unless you are taller than I am and can therefore get a more effective tilt going on, some residual wee may remain in the tube when you remove it. Oh yuck. Maybe not so ingenious. That was a new life experience anyway.

I met up with Mary, Kate and Liz from Sole Sisters and we hung out for half an hour or so until it was time to go into our allocated start pens, all chewing on various sports energy bars and supping at our bottles of water. The four of us seemed calm and ready to go and that remained the general air all around us. Already it was apparent that the event organisation was superb. There must have been thousands of runners in that starting area but it didn't feel overcrowded, it was clear where everything was and the queues for port-a-loos were long but not ridiculous as they are at some events. At around 9.45 a.m. we hugged and good lucked and went into the start pens based on our - or in my case Mark's - predicted finish times. They were just different numbered areas on the road. I had decided to take my phone with me in my sunglasses case that conveniently fits onto my gel belt so I sent a few last minute texts responding to well wishes from friends. When we all started to shuffle forwards towards the start line, I discarded my jacket and also my gloves as I had nowhere about my person to stash them - farewell, you served me well over the cold winter months - and tossed the bottle of water I had been dutifully sipping from too. It was time to run my longest ever run.

Despite being forewarned that the first few miles would be crowded and it would be difficult to get into a rhythm, I found that I could start running at my ideal pace straight away. I tried to stick between nine and ten-minute miles and, thankfully, I didn't find myself going too fast and having to pull back. Right from the start there were people lining the route and, having it emblazoned across my chest, calling out my name. There was music blasting out from people's front gardens and even a few live bands. If memory serves me right, I was finding hands held out for high fives even in the first mile. We ran past big Victorian or Edwardian houses (I'm not that hot on my architecture) set back from the road behind big gardens and then through an area of council houses (I'm guessing) with speed humps along the road manned by marshals with signs on poles saying Humps who were also bellowing out 'Humps!' and who sounded like the novelty of doing so had worn off some time before. In the first few miles I ran past a fairly senior looking gentleman using a crutch to get round and a young runner using two. Maybe he was determined to do the marathon in spite of an injury or perhaps he was trying for a different Guinness World Record? 'Rather them than me' I thought 'this will be hard enough on two fully functioning legs'.

After a few miles it became apparent that my bowels had let me down by not fully evacuating their contents earlier and I would have to look out for a course-side port-a-loo which I found a cluster of at around five miles into the run. It is disappointing time-wise to have to stop, but better than the indignity that might otherwise ensue. Negotiating the loos was a bit tricky, nobody in the gaggle of runners waiting wanted to stop for longer than they had to and hence all polite British queuing had gone out of the window. It didn't take me long to figure out that when a door opened I'd have to lunge for it otherwise I could be there a long time. I think I was stopped for about five minutes in all and thank goodness there was some toilet paper left. Too much information again?

After six miles the course takes you past the Royal Naval College and The Cutty Sark at Greenwich, which was pleasingly familiar territory from my time as a dance student in London, we used to hang out in Greenwich at the weekend sometimes. I think I should say at this point that overall the running and the crowds were proving to be my focal points so I'm sure I must have run past all sorts of other London landmarks that day without even noticing them. My account will be somewhat sparse in that respect but you can find out how the course weaves around iconic central London landmarks elsewhere.

Somewhere between miles seven and eight from her position in the crowd - where she had indeed been able to spot and photograph the back end of Mo Farah - Clare managed to pick me out of the mass of runners and turn my head in her direction with an ear-splitting, arms waving in the air cry of "ANDREAAA!!" She has got some pair of lungs on her. Apparently the poor runner next to me looked like she nearly jumped out of her skin. I love you for that though Clare; it was a brilliant moment.

I had decided when I started running that, uncharacteristically for me, I would employ some mental strategies, some mental trickery to help wile away the miles. To this end, I chose to mentally run the last eight miles of the distance first and get them out of the way. Anything over eighteen miles was more or less an unknown (having only done one run over that distance in training), so I figured that getting that out the way would leave me with something I knew I could do. At eight miles I said to myself, 'this is my race now, I know I can do this'. Yes it sounds daft, but if it works, so what?

At this point the running was very comfortable, my only irritation was my gel belt that kept swivelling on my waist because my top was made of such slippery synthetic material, cotton would have clung to it better I think and held it in place. It wouldn't have mattered except that the top of my race number was pinned to the belt so it kept getting all scrunched up as the belt moved round. It didn't take me long to decide that I couldn't rectify this situation so I'd just have to keep swivelling the belt back in the other direction again. Otherwise I was motoring along nicely enjoying the support from the crowds and trying to commit to memory interesting things I saw along the way. The handheld messages in the crowd that I enjoyed included.

- Run like the Zombies are after you!

- Feet hurting? That's because YOU'RE DOING IT!

- You're feeling like crap, but you look GREAT!

- May the course be with you!

The crowd's support in cheering, words of encouragement, banners, music and high fives was just amazing all the way round and definitely the highlight for me. I particularly loved high fiving the little tots in mummy or daddy's arms, they weren't really sure what was going on but it meant a lot to mum or dad when I made a special effort to gently slap the little hand being outstretched inside the parent's big one. Music being played live or over speakers was a great boost, just a little frustrating though that I'd start getting into a tune, maybe singing along then I'd be past, the uplifting sound fading into the distance, it would have been good to be able to carry it with me for a while longer.

My next goal after mile eight was to get through mile ten and attack the middle section of the race from ten to twenty. I know it's not the middle in numerical terms, but, given that the last six miles could feel like ten, it kind of makes sense. The mile markers are magnificent affairs, great scaffolding pillars at either side of the road be-topped with the appropriate mileage and joined with an arch of red and white balloons. They are easy to spot from way off and the feeling when the next one heaves into view ticking off another mile along the route is great. Just after mile twelve, the course takes you over Tower Bridge and this was probably the main landmark highlight for me, causing me to yell out in jubilation, "I'm running the London Marathon!" My cry was lost in the noise of the crowd and the pounding feet of runners, but I enjoyed it. Somewhere along the road leading up to the bridge I also got my most satisfying and resounding slap out of a high five, the kind you're always aiming for when you go for it, but then (nine times out of ten) you slightly miss and end up with something along a continuum from a complete all out miss (highly embarrassing) to that thing when you just feebly catch the edge of each others hands. High fives, they're a minefield.

As soon as I crossed the bridge I was aware that it was time to start scanning the crowd for my family support team and Jenny from Place2Be who planned to be somewhere around mile thirteen. I realised that I couldn't remember if I was supposed to be looking out for them on the right or left hand side of the road. I plumped for the right hand side (wrongly as it turned out) and began to scan the crowds for red and yellow Place2Be T shirts and the white baseball caps Clare had bought everyone with messages on them like 'My mum's running the London Marathon!' I scanned and scanned to no avail and around mile fourteen I decided that they'd just have to try and spot me and get my attention and I would get back to focussing on the running. If we'd missed each other, I thought, it didn't matter too much as we'd have a second chance when the course doubled back along the same stretch of road later.

After passing under the fourteen mile marker and running for what seemed like an excessively long time with no further marker coming into view, I started to think, 'this mile feels more like two, gosh it's really dragging now'. Then I spotted the sixteen-mile marker and realised, phew, it really was two miles after all, I must have run through the marker for fifteen without even noticing it. The miles coming up to twenty were getting a little tougher to run now, but I was still generally feeling good and comfortably maintaining a nice even pace. I had a weird and very painful spasm that shot through my left knee somewhere around this time leaving it feeling a bit weak for a minute or so but then it returned to normal. I've no idea what that was about. We ran through a tunnel at one point somewhere in the Isle of Dogs-Canary Wharf section of the course and just before I went into it I noticed that a good number of runners (mainly men) had pulled up and were stood at the side of the road stretching (or peeing). There were also considerably more people now taking walking breaks and the general energy level of the mass of runners was starting to drop tangibly. At around mile seventeen, I suddenly felt my own energy level go down and I became aware that I was feeling really hungry and empty. I tore open a gel and swallowed it as quickly as I could, availed myself of some jelly babies from the next person in the crowd I saw holding out a handful, and took a sports drink at the Lucozade station. That seemed to get me back to feeling tired but not completely sapped. My hips started to stiffen up around this time too so I tried to consciously relax them as I ran and this feeling also passed. As the going got tough, I took inspiration from thinking about Mark. I know that Mark was totally committed as a runner and would have run all the way and I wanted to do the same. If I was running the race for him, I had to do it in a way that would have earned his respect without walking and in a time that would count as good for a first-timer. I wasn't too sure what finish time I was heading towards at this point but I knew that things were going well and I still had plenty left in me for the final push. Running past my hotel just before the eighteen-mile marker and not being overwhelmed by any desire to jump the barriers and skip the last part of the race, I knew that I had this marathon business cracked.

This seems like a good point to pause and summarise how my hydration and nutrition worked out on the day. After doing my homework the night before, I had decided that I would use the four gels that my belt could hold at around miles six, twelve, eighteen and twenty three and that's pretty much how it worked out. I've always struggled to tear the tops off the gel packs without them remaining stubbornly attached at one end, so with my second gel I decided to get assertive and tear with extra force. Unfortunately the tab then tore off but also took the whole side of the pack with it and half of the gel shot out onto the road. Doh. I then got extremely sticky trying to consume the remaining gel out of what remained of the tattered packaging and I mean extremely sticky, we're talking a two year old eating a jam sandwich kind of sticky. With the drinks, I ended up doing something I never have before and running with a bottle in my hand for a lot of the time. I think it made me feel more secure knowing that I had a drink with me and I could just take a glug at regular intervals. One of the things that stuck in my mind from reading 'Keep on Running - The Highs and Lows of a Marathon Addict', was Phil Hewitt attributing the successful running of his first marathon (also London) and not hitting the wall to drinking little and often all the way round. Also, it wasn't bothering me at all to hold onto the bottle and run with it as I'd thought it might beforehand. I had planned to take a few swigs and toss the bottles to one side, which is accepted race practice. I'm going out on a limb here, but I'm sure that when your core muscles aren't strong a little thing like holding a bottle can feel really awkward because the weight throws your body off centre, but now that I have a strong core from all my training it didn't have that effect. I used the drink stations when my bottle was getting too empty or I wanted to change from water to a sports drink and with new found marathon purposefulness I would hold my arm out like I was signalling to turn the corner on a bicycle, hand ready to receive a bottle, in full expectation that one of the volunteers manning the stations would see and respond, my body language saying, 'Lay some hydration on me. There is no timidity about me today, I'm a marathon runner now!'

After passing twenty miles, the countdown was on, counting backwards from six to zero, the equivalent of an easy midweek run. Yes, mental trickery again and only easy after you've been marathon training for months. Just after twenty-one miles the course again joins with the thirteen to fourteen miles section going in the opposite direction and it was time to start looking out for my support team again. Realising my earlier mistake, I knew which side to look this time but still couldn't spot them and had just given up looking when Clare's impressive hail cut through the general noise again and I just about had time before sweeping past to raise my arm in acknowledgement in their general direction, captured on camera by Keziah. Somewhere between miles twenty and twenty-three I think (if memory serves me right) we ran through another tunnel, which for that day had been named the 'Lucozade Tunnel of Dig Deep'. All through the tunnel there were giant paper lanterns each lit up and bearing an inspirational message, variations on the theme of 'You can do it!' backed up by some pumping music.

In the final three miles the crowd support and noise became supercharged and excitement was building for the finish. As runners - and I imagine I speak for most of us - we were really flagging by now and the crowd and their well wishes made a huge difference. People had been calling out my name at regular intervals all the way round with a wonderful variety of accents and pronunciations and I particularly lapped up the attention at this point. The only versions I wasn't sure about were "Andree!" (maybe they couldn't see the final 'a'?) and the addition of "Good effort!" Good effort? That might as well be, "You're pretty slow, but good on you for trying!" I find that a bit patronising. Please, if you find yourself in a crowd of supporters one day, substitute that phrase for something more upbeat along the lines of, "You're doing amazingly!" It has more syllables and takes a bit more breath I grant you, but it rings better in the ears of a weary marathon runner (well, this one anyway). Those last three miles were by far the hardest and my pace started to really tail off, but I knew how close to the finish I was and there was no way I was going to give in and walk now. A lady running in a wedding dress came alongside me and was getting all you would expect from the male portion of the crowd, "Will you marry me?", "I do", etc. She must have had that all the way round and had probably tuned out by that point. As we ran along Victoria Embankment I nearly choked on my water but I couldn't seem to manage a normal cough from my throat and some strange seal-like barking noise emerged from what felt like the depths of my lungs. It is bizarre what marathon running does to your body. Other hazardous incidents during the 26.2 miles included nearly twisting my ankle on the raised road markings of a mini roundabout, tripping over another runner's foot - tsk, she cut me up - and only stopping myself from falling over completely by using the runner in front of me as a set of human buffers (my apologies whoever you were), getting my feet tangled up in a plastic bag, and getting elbow chopped on the shoulders by the pumping arms of taller male runners when we were bunched closely together in certain places around the course (painful). Clearly marathon running is hazardous to one's health in more ways than you might imagine.

Suddenly The Houses of Parliament came into view in front of us and on reaching them we turned right and headed towards Buckingham Palace. I knew how close I was to the end but in spite of this the final mile was by far the hardest. Had it not been the final mile I would have been seriously tempted to walk given how I felt but there was no way on earth I was even entertaining that notion now no matter how exhausted I was. The banners in the middle of the road counting down 800 metres, 600 metres, 385 yards (go and do your marathon homework) and 200 metres to the finish line only served to make this last bit even more torturous. What do you mean *only* 800 metres to go? That's a really long way right now! But finally we turned right again into The

Mall, the finishing gantry was in view and then I was crossing the timing mats underneath it and having a medal placed around my neck. I DID IT! And I ran all the way. My official finishing time was a very satisfying 4:25:42. Wow, I had run the London Marathon!

On stopping, my first reactions were, 'Phew, thank goodness I can stop running now', 'Ouch, my feet are killing me', and, 'Ouch, my shoulders are killing me almost as much as my feet'. I really don't think I do finish line euphoria because this would surely have been a fitting moment for it, I just do finish line relief. I staggered - not because I was feeling wobbly, but because my feet were hurting so much - through the official photograph-with-your-medal bit and picked up my goody bag and my kit bag from the lorry (which I could then barely carry because my shoulders were hurting so much) and started heading towards the meet and greet area where I was going to wait near the letter G for Pete, Clare, mum and the children. I say started because I didn't make it in one go, it was so uncomfortable to walk that I had to sit down for ten minutes at the base of a tree to rest before I could go the full distance. Sitting down and standing up again are no mean feat in themselves after a long run and have potential for some good comedy moments. Runners give each other sympathetic smiles as they tentatively attempt these difficult manoeuvres often accompanied by a groan of pain.

Partially revived by a few minutes off my pins and by eating the apple in my goody bag - it tasted *so* good - I managed to make it to the big G in Horse Guards Parade and found an empty spot in front of a cannon to sit down and text the family. A guy calling himself Marathon man, who is hoping to make a world record for marathon running (maybe for the most consecutive marathons run) and always runs in a suit like Superman's with an M on the front instead of the S, happened to sit down beside me and asked how my marathon had gone. On hearing that it was my first he asked if he could film an interview with me on his iPhone and I obliged (he was making a collection of interviews with first-time marathon runners he has met on his travels) telling him the story of how I'd come to be running that day. After ten minutes or so my family (Clare counts as such too) arrived and there were big hugs and congratulations from everyone. My children were excited and my accompanying adults were looking a little ragged around the edges. It is no mean feat keeping a group together on the Underground and in the crowds (and in the crowds on the Underground).

Once toilet queues had been braved by mum and Clare plus various children, my feet had been manipulated and massaged by Pete and everyone was ready to face the Underground once again, we made for Paddington for something to eat before the family caught their train back to Bristol at 7.30 p.m. Having had some rest I now felt fine to walk and I knew it was advisable to do so rather than stopping still for too long and allowing everything to seize up. At the station our goodbyes were said until the following day, then Sam and I headed back to the hotel at Canary Wharf together ready for his thirteenth birthday outing the following day.

So, I did it. That crazy big marathon idea that had begun to germinate last summer had come to fruition and what a truly amazing experience it had been. Topping the amazingness charts would be and in no particulate order:

- **The crowds of spectators and runners.** I've been asked since if I ran the marathon with anyone else on the day. Yep, about 34,000 other runners and 26.2 miles worth of spectators. There were a few of us you might say. I felt really supported all the way round. The crowd's passion was equivalent to us being a super-sized Team GB at the Olympics last summer and we were cheered and encouraged from the start right through to the finish line.

- **The event organisation.** Phenomenal.

- **My training paying off.** In terms of the running alone, I had my best ever race experience. There was never a point where I doubted that I would get round. It was so satisfying to know that I'd run the whole way and achieved a very respectable time for a first marathon. All those freezing winter runs had been worthwhile. Here are some of my race statistics to illustrate the respectability of my effort (with thanks Runpix who compile them): I came 16,672 out of 34,217 finishers (pretty much bang in the middle of the field). I came 33% of the way down the field of female runners (40% for the specific category of female runners aged 40-44). My average speed was 5.9 mph. Finally, and I particularly enjoy this one, in the last 7k I overtook 803 runners and 150 overtook me.

- **The connection I felt with other runners.** I think I spent the whole journey between Paddington and South Quay with Sam that evening exchanging experiences with different people and chatting with complete ease. I even met someone who'd just returned from running the Hamburg marathon the same day and we compared medals, race T-shirts and goody bag contents.

- **The satisfaction of achieving my goals.** I set my feet on a course of action (in this case very literally) that seemed a huge feat (not so literally, or illiterately, there, I don't have huge feet) and I achieved all I wanted to. Thank you Mark for inspiring me to reach for something bigger than I ever imagined I had in me. You live on in the impact you had, and continue to have, in the lives and work of others and in running your marathon - and maybe more of my own in the future, who knows - I feel I have forged a connection with you that transcends the distance we felt in life.

Journal Entry 29 – 29th May 2013

Life After the Marathon

It's been over five weeks since running the marathon and I have allowed the dust to settle and some life to pass under the bridge before starting to write this entry. Enough time to have something to say in addition to, 'Ooh, I ache'.

Sam and I managed our visit to The Natural History Museum on the day after the marathon with considerably more ease than I had imagined. I didn't have to plead for the use of a wheelchair (a possibility that I had considered out loud beforehand and not entirely in jest). Sam did have to wander round the museum on his own more by the time the afternoon came though whilst I took the weight off my feet in the cafe, as my energy levels had dropped through the floor. I could have used my post-marathon fatigue as a perfectly valid ready-made excuse not to get up on my feet again and walk through the dinosaur gallery for the umpteenth time lingering over every exhibit, but I tried not to milk it too much as it meant a lot to Sam for us to have a special day together and for me to share in the things that he loves. Walking down the stairs at the museum became noticeably more uncomfortable as the day wore on (that always seems to be the thing that gets you most after a race) and I started having to do the take-one-step-down-and-let-the-other-foot-catch-up thing, or alternatively go down sideways. I didn't resort to bumping downstairs on my bottom however (the final resort if all other options are too painful), that would have been a little too conspicuous for Sam to cope with I imagine. In retrospect I'm not sure why I didn't just use the lift, I must have subconsciously felt that my protesting muscles were a trophy of the previous day's effort to be prized in all their painful glory. Back in Bristol on Tuesday I had the sports massage that my friend Petra had booked for me as a well-done present. The therapist knew her stuff, she managed to find all the most tender muscles without my direction and give them a good working over. Er, thanks I think.

So, how was my post-marathon recovery overall? Sure, naturally my muscles were sore, but not so bad that I couldn't walk around normally (stairs notwithstanding). I don't think anyone would have seen obvious external signs of the rigours I'd just put myself through. My hamstrings, quadriceps and calves were the main places I hurt, my hamstrings taking the longest to fully recover at around a week. I also had a mysterious narrow band of soreness across my back below my shoulder blades. Maybe that was from pumping my arms for 26.2 miles or from the tension of clutching a water bottle much of the way round? Well those are my best guesses anyway.

All in all, I'd say that my recovery from the more acute effects of my marathon effort was fairly speedy. I deliberately didn't run at all for ten days, even though driving around the streets I've run along so many times recently had me itching to get my trainers on again. I opted instead for a few swimming sessions. Actually that's exaggerating, truthfully one proper swim and one trip to the pool with the children that involved very little swimming more pretending under duress to be a shark.

For a good week or so after the marathon I felt like I was entitled to a standing ovation in every friendship situation I went into, actually any situation at all really including those involving complete strangers. Surely what I'd achieved must have left a detectable aura around me? Disappointingly that response wasn't forthcoming but those who knew I'd run the marathon were suitably impressed that I was able to walk around normally - i.e. that I wasn't a complete hobbling wreck - and were happy to humour me and admire my medal which I made sure I carried in my handbag for a full week. There were a lot of comments about the medal looking like a Jim'll Fix It badge owing to the shape and ribbon colour. A note to the organisers - In future perhaps avoid oblong shaped medals on red ribbons as the association for my generation is very powerful and it does rather steal one's thunder to have person after person say, "Ooh, is that your medal? It looks like a Jim'll Fix It badge". Jim did not fix it for me, I did it all myself.

My longer-term post-marathon recovery has been more of an issue than the immediate aches and pains. I have had more discomfort under the ball of my left foot, like the niggle that first developed on the long runs in training. Fortunately this didn't trouble me when I ran the marathon, but on my first run back after those ten days off - in retrospect I think this was maybe too soon to be running again - it was really painful after three miles. I took a further nine days off before my next attempt and did some ginger footbaths in the evenings and now it seems ok to run on. Not completely back to normal yet, but not painful anymore either. This is the foot on which I broke a toe which may be relevant, although since reading 'Born to Run' by Christopher McDougall, I'm wondering if there might be another cause, but I'll return to that thought in a few paragraphs time.

In that slightly frustrating period of not being able to run, feeling at peak fitness and unable to keep training, I did something I haven't done for years and got on a bicycle. Me and bikes have never been best of friends as I've always felt a bit wobbly on two wheels, but some things improve with age and general levels of confidence in life and this principle appears, for me anyway, to apply to bike riding and also to my ability to catch. It's amazing how needing to catch food items in glass jars as they hurl themselves out of my untidy overstuffed kitchen cupboards has sharpened my reflexes. In terms of time management, it's an advantage to get to the jar of Piccalilli (or other suicidal condiment) before it hits the deck, smashes and splatters it's contents far and wide. It's just a shame I had to go through all those years of terror in the school playground dreading the rounders ball being batted in my direction, all eyes on me as it sailed towards my outstretched arms in the statistical likelihood of being fumbled and dropped (I'm guessing I'm not alone in that experience) before discovering my latent ability to make a good catch even with my left hand. I still throw like a girl though; I haven't found a remedy for that one yet.

Now that the marathon after-effects have subsided, I am aiming to run three times a week, runs of between three and six miles at the moment. I am hoping over the next couple of weeks to get back to a long run of around ten miles every fortnight or so, but I think it best to build up to that slowly by adding an extra mile each time I do a longer run as, just as in my marathon training, too much of a jump in distance could be a recipe for injury in this recovery period. In terms of my overall running fitness post-marathon, my experience has been mixed. Straight away it was clear that my average pace for a run has improved noticeably now often being under nine minute miles, but for a good few weeks my breathing felt really laboured when I ran as if all of the muscles involved had got totally out of shape and had forgotten that they got me through a marathon only a month back. My legs have felt good though, no problems there at all.

The most exciting developments with my running since I started out on my marathon journey are that (a) I can now most definitely run without walking breaks, even for 26.2 miles - not necessarily without toilet breaks though - and (b) I now look forward to going out for a run on my own. I have discovered enjoyment in the act of running itself and I enjoy the way a familiar route changes according to the time of day, the season and the weather. Maybe for me I just needed to reach a higher level of fitness before I could be comfortable to see running - even when I'm puffing and panting and my muscles are screaming at me - as a pleasurable act in itself. It is great to have got to that place as I wasn't sure I ever would, so I hope I won't forfeit it by letting myself slide back into being a once a week runner. I hope running will become something that's an integral part of looking after myself, like brushing my teeth, although I stop the parallel short of running twice a day. My new found enjoyment was evidenced to myself in a five mile morning run being the way I chose to start the day of my 42nd birthday, even though it meant getting up extra early. I certainly wouldn't have made that choice a year ago.

I've only managed one run with my club since the marathon owing to the three recovery weeks I took and, since Easter, a clash with the time of my eldest daughter's swimming club. On that club night I opted to run with the fast six-mile group and I struggled. I am not fast enough to stay at the front of the pack with that group, but out of pride - well I am a marathon runner now - I tried to and it nearly killed me. Trying to run up Winterbourne Hill and keep pace with super-fit Rebecca - who ran her first marathon in Manchester a week after mine in London in less than four hours - was possibly not a good judgement call. Sole Sisters have had a record year for marathon runners (London, Manchester and Brighton marathons amongst others both at home and abroad) and a good handful of the ladies have also managed to run theirs in under four hours. Inspirational. I'd probably have to follow their examples and get some regular cross-training sessions going if I want to get that fast. Cross-training (referring to alternative forms of exercise to build strength in particular muscle groups, not obsessive use of the cross-training machine in the gym) feels like a whole other ball game to me though. I can't even begin to think how it could fit into my week. For a while last year when I was getting over a running injury I enjoyed doing an intense twenty minute daily burst of exercise with a Jillian Michaels DVD at home which felt really beneficial, but I eventually got put off by the permanent audience of four kids spectating from the sofa. It wouldn't have surprised me if they'd started holding up scorecards. And, no, our living room isn't big enough for me to have turned the experience into a home education exercise class.

So, as my marathon experience obviously hasn't put me off running forever, would I run another marathon? Well, seeing as I was to be found at 1.30 a.m. on the 29th April filling out online ballot entries for London 2014 for myself, Clare and Graham, I guess that would have to be a yes. I can't envisage punctuating my running year with marathons in the way that I have with spring and autumn half-marathons, but if an opportunity comes up to enter an interesting event in the future then I may go for it. Interesting for me would be a marathon that gives me an excuse to visit an exciting city at home or abroad that I've never been to before, or to run in a totally new situation (like countryside instead of city). The undulations of Dartmoor Vale Marathon with Graham and Nick in October is a possibility that has been put to me. At the moment I'm undecided. It partly depends on how my nigglesome foot holds up when I attempt some longer runs again over the next few weeks, as training would need to start for it soon. In terms of half-marathons, I will probably run an autumn one (not sure which yet though) and I have volunteered to run Bath next spring with another of my many brothers, Jamie, to raise money for the local charity Mentoring+ that he works for.

In the two weeks after the marathon a flurry of donations for Place2Be came in through my Just Giving page taking me to my target of £1000 and beyond, which was really satisfying. Friends had seen from posts on Facebook that I'd actually done it and responded with their credit cards. I hadn't anticipated so many people making donations after the event. Clare was keen for me to apply for a place to run London marathon for a charity next year (we're more likely to be able to do it this way than hoping on getting a ballot place), but I'm not sure myself. It is hard asking your circle of friends and family to dip into their pockets again and again. I'm really glad that Place2Be have benefitted this time though, as £1000 will fund one hundred one-to-one counselling sessions for children in schools who are struggling and in need of support.

For a month or so after the marathon my desire to devour running related reading matter abated considerably and was limited to the latest issue of Women's Running. But then on a visit to our local library, my eye fell on a prominent display of sports books and I was off again coming home with copies of the aforementioned Born to Run and 'Running with the Kenyans' by Adharanand Finn. I galloped (or to stay with the theme I should perhaps say sprinted) through the fascinating Born to Run, a book length piece of hands-on (or rather feet-on) investigative journalism about injury free running, the Tarahumara people of the Mexican Barrancas and ultra running. This book gives really interesting insights into various aspects of running including what it takes to be an ultra runner (someone who runs distances greater than a marathon) and whether modern running shoes are doing us more harm than good. Hence me pondering afresh the reason for my uncomfortable left foot.

On ultra running, this is McDougall talking about Ann Trason.

"One Saturday, Ann got up early and ran twenty miles. She relaxed over breakfast, then headed back out for twenty more. She had some plumbing chores around the house, so after finishing run No. 2, she hauled out her toolbox and got to work. By the end of the day, she was pretty pleased with herself; she'd run forty miles and taken care of a messy job on her own. So as a reward, she treated herself to another fifteen miles...of course her friends didn't get it because they'd never broken through. For them, running was a miserable two miles motivated solely by size 6 jeans: get on the scale, get depressed, get your headphones on, and get it over with. But you can't muscle through a five-hour run that way; you have to relax into it, like easing your body into a hot

bath, until it no longer resists the shock and begins to enjoy it...."You have to be in tune with your body, and know when you can push it and when to back off" ".

Despite having successfully taken on the marathon distance myself, I currently have no desire to venture into ultra running territory. But I do relate to the observation about dutiful running. When running is done through gritted teeth purely for the results, it can be a miserable experience. Of course you'd want to block that out with some loud tunes on the iPod. But when you engage with all the signals your body is giving you as you run, and in between runs, and work with it, always aiming to run better (not necessarily faster, but smoother and more pain and injury free), then, as I have found, it can become a pleasure and you really can go on and on and on and on.

On running shoes and injuries, this from Born to Run:

"Every year, anywhere from 65 to 80 percent of all runners suffer an injury. That's nearly every runner, every single year. No matter who you are, no matter how you run, your odds of getting hurt are the same.... Lucky for us though, we live in a golden age of technology. Running-shoe companies have had a quarter century to perfect their designs, so logically, the injury rate must be in free fall by now.... Right? Sorry... In fact, there's no evidence that running shoes are any help at all in injury prevention."

McDougall goes on, citing studies and observations from experts involved in running and coaching.

"[According to one study] Runners wearing top-of-the-line shoes are 123 percent more likely to get injured than runners in cheap shoes.... Your legs and feet instinctively come down hard when they sense something squishy underfoot. When you run in cushioned shoes, your feet are pushing through the soles in search of a hard, stable platform... "The deconditioned musculature of

the foot is the greatest issue leading to injury..." Hartmann said.... *"Blueprint your feet, and you'll find a marvel that engineers have been trying to match for centuries."*

In other words, less is more and nothing at all (barefoot running) may be the best option of all, so maybe I need to go back to those T K Maxx £29.99 trainers with less cushioned soles and give them another go to clear up my remaining foot niggles.

I am fascinated by what I've found out along my journey about how well our bodies are designed for running. Injury-free running in the long-term really is possible it would seem if we recognise what an amazing vehicle we inhabit and then set out to understand how best to work with it for optimal running efficiency. As time goes on I am evermore amazed at the running feats I can achieve with my (although I'm sad to admit it) middle-aged body. I don't think it responds so very differently to training as the body of a young person would. Life and running can definitely begin at forty. Of course, on the flip side, when we realise how incredible our bodies are it then becomes apparent that we can and often do take them so much for granted. We inflict some pretty hefty abuse on them. It's the equivalent of owning a state-of-the-art Ferrari but treating it with the little care we might show a beat-up fifteen year old banger scraping through it's MOT for another year's worth (you hope) of school runs and grocery shopping.

As my account draws to a close, it's time to reflect on whether running a marathon has changed me. A large chunk of the final chapter of The Non-Runner's Marathon Trainer is devoted to accounts from first time marathon runners who all say that their outlook on life is different for having experienced both the journey and the accomplishment. My answer would have to be that I am in a different place now to this time last year not just because of the achievement of running a marathon but also because taking on the challenge and doing something completely new has given me an opportunity to lift up my eyes from the last thirteen years of marriage, producing and caring for children, and managing a household, to consider the person I've become. There is no doubt that I am now a fitter, healthier person physically and there are reserves of mental courage and tenacity that I have had to discover in myself to run long distances, but I've come to realise that other aspects of my life are in need of a serious overhaul too. I have allowed my personal life to stagnate and I find myself desperate to get the waters of joy, truth and love flowing again not just for my own sake but also for the sake of all those whose lives are touched by mine. So for me, the more important journey now needs to be embraced. Comparatively speaking it was straightforward to train for and run a marathon. I chose a plan to follow, put in the work and got the result I wanted. Job done as they say. Life changes around my inner self and my relationships feel far more messy and uncertain, but if engaged with will I think ultimately be as rewarding and arguably more worthwhile. We can go through our whole lives running away from or ignoring our personal pain and struggles and consequently not living life to the full, or we can summon all our courage, face up to difficult things and breakthrough to more abundant living. It may be that Mark's legacy to me, and to all the children who will be helped by the donations to Place2Be, is an opportunity to face up to and overcome our troubles. Mark may not have been able to make peace with his own internal struggles, but he wanted others to have the opportunity to do so and ideally early in life.

To revisit a theme from entry 22 and consider further the place that running occupied in Mark's later life, maybe I now better understand why running can become such a pivotal part of our experience of well being, besides the physical benefits it brings. Actually it suddenly seems obvious. We live in a world where we have to grapple daily with huge uncertainties, some are constants and some more specific to our personal circumstances and the political and social climate we are living in. Will I be made redundant in the next round of cuts? Can I find a job that

I find fulfilling? Will I ever be free from debt? Will my kids do well in life or will they go off the rails? Will cancer that has taken the lives of so many people close to me come knocking again? Will my marriage go the distance? Will I find someone special to share my life with? Will I like where I find myself in 10 years time? Etc., etc. Add in the uncertainties you grapple with. Sometimes the unanswered questions that hang over us are deep ones that signify our need to understand our place in the universe. For many of us, amidst the uncertainties and insecurity of life, running gives us a way to set and achieve our own goals and measure our success independently of anyone and anything else. We don't have to compete against anyone but ourselves unless we want to and we can choose the standards by which we measure our progress and indeed define what constitutes success to us. Pretty much anyone, health issues notwithstanding, can follow a training plan at his or her chosen level and achieve a tangible result at the end of it. So running gives us the opportunity for mastery in at least one sphere of life.

Big organised running events give us an opportunity to come together with fellow running enthusiasts and test our fitness and progress at regular intervals through the year and everyone comes away with a prize that celebrates their individual effort (a medal, a T shirt, a goody bag). Contemplating and writing this section brought to mind a comment the fast-for-age lady had made whilst Clare and I were chatting to her in Costa before the marathon. She said, as I remember, "Parkruns are like a new religion really, it's quite scary the communities that have developed around them". We are all looking for things that enable us to feel like we have a handle on this messy old life and I think that is part of the reason we run, it gives us an area we can feel in control of. I think it's important to acknowledge though, as an extension of this thought, that even though running is a healthy pursuit overall, for some it can become something that tips over into being an unhealthy obsession. I guess it's all about balance at the end of the day, as with most things in life.

Well, that's a subject for me to continue mulling on as I continue on my own running journey. In the meantime, as I finally - many weeks later - come to the end of this marathon-length entry, I am on week three of my training for Dartmoor Vale Marathon in the autumn. I was persuaded. I have a sixteen-mile long run tomorrow. My training has definitely jumped up a level from last time and I'm running stronger, faster and, so far, foot-niggle free, thanks (I think) to my transition into a more minimalist style of running shoe. It feels very different to be training for marathon number two as it doesn't hold the meaning that my first did, or the glamour of London, and running four times a week again feels like a big commitment, but I'm treating it as something of an experiment on various levels - can I run a marathon faster? Do I like the distance or was London a one-off, never to be replicated, wonderful experience? - And I'll see how it goes...

Beyond London – Autumn 2013

Training for and Running My Second Marathon

Well it turned out that London marathon went so well for me that I could actually contemplate doing it all over again and so I did six months later. On 20th October 2013 I ran my second marathon, Dartmoor Vale. Feeling so amazingly fit after all my training for London, it seemed like the best way to remain committed to running regularly and to maintain that condition was to enter an autumn marathon. Looking back on that period of my life from a few years further down the road, that sounds like a barmy kind of thinking. I must been overtaken by some sort of marathon induced madness. Don't worry; it is possible to be a good strong runner without entering an arduous six-monthly cycle of marathon running. But at that time I think I'd got hooked on the idea of staying at my peak level of running fitness and setting another marathon goal seemed the only way to achieve it.

It took a bit of deliberation between running partner Graham and myself before we reached a decision on which marathon to enter together. Not being too well off financially (as you may have already realised from my entries about buying bargain running gear), the entrance fee was one of the biggest factors under consideration. Racing can be an expensive business and some of the marathons on our shortlist had entry fees of £60 and we also noticed that in the event of deferment the fees were not always transferable. In the end we chose Dartmoor Vale marathon for it's reasonable entry price, hilly challenges and the opportunity to join running friend Nick as he entered for his second year (he came in fifth overall both times, coming in in just over three hours). Here is a collection of memories, experiences, highlights and low points from training for and running marathon number two. This may feel rather brief and fragmented after the flow and detail of my entries about training for and running London marathon but I hope that it is enough to give a little insight into the next phase of my running journey.

The Training

Hills:

An unexpected and exciting development from all my training for London was that as soon as I started my second cycle of marathon training I found that I had the strength to run hills confidently. For the first time since I began running, I felt strong enough to really power my way up long and steep hills which was an amazing feeling, particularly when I looked back and re-membered the dread and terror which even a slight incline used to provoke in me as a beginner. I heartily recommend embracing the hills rather than avoiding them, you will conquer them as your general level of fitness increases and, when you do, you will also feel on top of the world. We deliberately ran at least one steep hill on each long training run to prepare for those we had been forewarned that we would encounter on the Dartmoor Vale course.

Partnership:

In addition to my newfound hill prowess, I found that I was running faster overall, which, whilst exhilarating for me, threw up new challenges in terms of training with a partner. Graham was having a tough time with marathon training this time around as long working hours were taking a significant toll on his energy levels for running so it felt like the tables had turned and in this season I was the stronger of the two of us. So now I was faced with the conundrum that Graham had handled with such equanimity a few months before when we began to run together regularly; that being, when you run with a partner and you find that you are wanting to go at different paces, do you find a compromise because you value the partnership or do you put your own training ambitions first and either ditch your partner or drag them along with you at a pace that they are finding miserable and uncomfortable? I found that I had to work at discerning when a "You go ahead, don't wait for me" was genuine and when it might actually really mean, " For goodness sake, have a heart and slow down!" If I thought I had discerned correctly I realised there was still a decision for me to make as to whether to return the consideration that Graham had shown me when he was the stronger partner or to selfishly pursue what I wanted for myself. These are the challenges and considerations in being a good running partner. Sometimes (unless you are a perfect running match all the time) you do have to be prepared to either put the brakes on or step up your game a little. Through different times and seasons there is ideally some give and take on both sides and each person brings something that benefits the other. I learnt that I think Graham is better at all of this than I am.

Long runs:

I was able to do the long training runs together with Graham all the way through our sixteen weeks of marathon training. Following a different training schedule to the one I chose for London, we started the programme of long runs at a high mileage straight away and built up quickly very early on in the programme, occasionally having a lower mileage rest week. This may have been unwise as a I did experience more uncomfortable niggles throughout my training and in hindsight I realised that I would do better to stick with a more gradual approach another time.

Fitting it all in:

Fitting all the weekly runs in around family life took greater flexibility and determination this time around as my children's extra-curricular activities had just begun to crowd out more of the week. In particular I remember two 6.30 a.m. starts for Saturday long runs (of sixteen and eighteen miles) so that I was available to officiate at swimming galas for my daughter Keziah's club later the same morning. Standing on my feet for three hours in the humid environment of a packed swimming pool with clipboard and stopwatch in hand having already pounded through all those miles I have to admit that I felt like a little smug; 'How amazing am I?' I thought to myself.

Rewards:

Aside from the pure functionality of racking up the training miles and getting the body and mind marathon-ready again, there were some extra rewards from all the hours spent pounding the pavements. We tried out and enjoyed new running routes (including new monster hills), I discovered the peacefulness of choosing routes on my mid-week runs alone that took me away from the traffic wherever possible, and there were many funny and bizarre moments like coming to the aid of an escaped Chihuahua in a pink diamanté studded collar running along a main road against the flow of traffic. The absolute highlight was smashing my half-marathon PB by nine minutes five weeks before Dartmoor Vale marathon, running the Bristol course on September 15th 2013 in 1:52, a time that I had never even dreamt that I could achieve. The training intensity needed for a new half-marathon PB sneaks in under the radar with marathon training. I love that. An excellent and unexpected reward.

The training miles:

I missed the personal significance of training for London 2013 and the unique blend of excitement and nervous anticipation that came with preparing for my very first marathon. Training for Dartmoor was more about hard work and less about the meaning and prestige. Looking back, I'm quite amazed and encouraged that I managed to maintain the training without such big incentives, without even a sticker chart in fact. In terms of the training, I wouldn't say that I got casual, but there was some free-styling in the sense that I guessed the kind of distances I thought I should be aiming for at any particular point (based on last time) rather than following a specific plan. One major departure was taking a whole week off from training when we went to see family in Lincolnshire in the summer and hoping this would allow time for some niggles to settle down. Otherwise I was pretty faithful in getting out for four training runs a week and going early in the morning to avoid the heat of the day (I definitely favour winter running conditions).

Niggles:

I found that my left foot and knee were not happy with the training demands. It always seems to be my left side that gives me problems, I'm not sure why. I had some discomfort and stiffness on the inside of my knee in between runs (although it never bothered me when I actually was running) and also different niggles working their way around that foot, nothing that I would put in the category of a definite injury, but nevertheless bothersome and frustrating. In the last week before the marathon, I experienced some stiffness on the outside of my left ankle and at this point, after weeks of training through one niggle or the other, I actually considered pulling out of the marathon. In retrospect (and being back to 100% running fitness), I can only think that my body is still going through the process of adjusting to the volume of training I do both since I became a runner and since progressing to marathon running. So far, despite my worries, all these aches and pains have in fact passed after a few weeks. I think I probably scared myself by reading too many stories about running injuries so every new twinge felt like it could be a potential marathon-stopper, but training since Dartmoor and seeing all the niggles pass into memory has given me new confidence that not every prickle of discomfort we feel as runners heralds the arrival of a major injury.

Shoes:

Having read about high-tech running shoes and the possible relationship with running injuries, and with the discomfort I experienced under the ball of my left foot during the later stages of my training for London, I decided to experimentally make the switch to a fairly minimalist pair of shoes for most of my training for Dartmoor. The new running shoes were pretty flat and nice and roomy and flexible around the forefoot. My foot problem resolved completely. Given all the other little niggles I went on to experience I definitely couldn't say that the change of shoes was a cure-all - who knows, maybe my foot soreness just would've healed anyway - but either way I felt that more minimal running shoes were the way forward for me. Currently I am running in a fairly simple pair of trainers that whilst not quite so minimal as the pair I trained for Dartmoor in are definitely more towards that end of the spectrum and they are my favourite pair to date (in fact they are the £29.99 T K Maxx bargain K Swiss pair I bought during my training for London then had a wobble about using at that point in time).

Strava:

Nick introduced me to the free online training tool Strava. I upload data from my Garmin running watch to my personal profile on the site and it creates a training log for me. Based on the data from a running watch or phone with appropriate app installed, Strava maps out individual runs, awards 'cups' for PBs over all distances and over particular named sections on the map (a paying 'premium' member can highlight and name a section of or a whole route they run on regularly and all other members running this are then placed on a leaderboard according to their time), mile splits are given for each run, weekly mileage recorded and more. Members can connect with each other, comment on each other's runs and award 'kudos' if they see fit. There is something very satisfying about logging runs on my Strava profile and seeing the column of my weekly mileage bar chart rise, and the icing on the cake is being awarded a cup for breaking a course record or beating a previous PB. Using the site certainly enhances my training experience in-between events, the only glitch being that my Garmin that has started to behave somewhat erratically, losing signal at inopportune moments, leading to some interesting statistics, generally in my favour; apparently I ran a mile of Bristol half-marathon in somewhere around four minutes!

The Marathon in Brief:

The course: Two laps on country roads. Undulations in abundance (long slow ones). Hills (including a long, steep, goes-on-forever one). More hills.

The weather: Mild, grey and mostly dry apart from a torrential soak-you-through-to-the-skin-and-blow-you-about-a-bit-at-the-same-time ten-minute downpour somewhere around mile twenty.

The puddle: A nice deep one spanning a single-track road from hedgerow to hedgerow which runners had no choice but to splosh through on both laps meaning their shoes became completely waterlogged.

Most amusing moment: A chap fifty metres ahead of me sounding off at top volume and shaking his fist at the torrential rain shower. I don't think he knew I was behind him, he thought he was alone and unobserved on a quiet country road.

The state of my feet afterwards: Wrinkled, soggy and muddy. The mud had penetrated through my shoes and my socks. One small blister.

The hardest bits: The first ten miles, as I felt out of sorts with my running after weeks of niggles and consequently nervous that I wouldn't be able to go the distance. All the hills on the second lap, which I mostly walked up because I knew I'd expend too much energy otherwise and struggle to finish the course. The last mile, because it felt like soooo much further than a mile, but I did still manage a sprint finish as a show of strength for the small crowd of spectators.

The marshals: Lovely Rotary Club members and friends. Warm, friendly and encouraging.

The spectators: Apart from at the start and finish, a scant handful.

The post-race goodies: A good quality medal, a technical T-shirt, bottle of water and a KitKat.

The water stations: Water in plastic cups - tricky to drink whilst running. I was glad I'd taken my own water bottle.

The camaraderie: Lots of support from fellow marathon runners, in particular very gracious responses to being overtaken, many offering a "Well done" or a "You're doing well". (Yes, I am sneaking in a little brag there). I also enjoyed a few miles of run/walk and chat with another runner close to the end after we both decided to walk one of the hills on the second lap to conserve energy.

My time: 4:25:45. Only three seconds slower than my time for London on a massively harder course.

My favourite moments: Finding the elusive flow at several points, even in the final tired few miles. My name being called over the speakers as I crossed the finish line. The view from the top of the really steep hill. Leaving the roads where we were running alongside traffic to run the quiet countryside single-track road section of the course. Getting through the psychologically difficult first lap and onto the second lap and knowing I would be able to finish.

Hydration & nutrition: Bang on. Four energy gels, water and a couple of glucose tablets in the last few miles.

The toilets: Only available at the start/finish, meaning I had to hop over a stile and go in a field on the way round.

Hardness rating: According to an online running forum Dartmoor Vale is a 4 out of 5 marathon course (5 being the hardest). The same forum rates London as a 1.5.

Hitting the wall: After a difficult training run-up Graham started out well on the day, but around miles 16-18 suddenly felt like his muscles were tightening up and had to stop and evaluate whether he could go on. At this point we separated - it was a "You go ahead, don't wait for me" moment. Graham tells me that he shed tears of frustration but resolved to finish the course of even if he had to walk. There can't have been too much walking because he still finished in 4:43. That man knows how to dig deep. Respect.

Would I do this course again?: Probably not. Something flatter another time.

Making it a Marathon Hat-Trick

Women's Running magazine has a lot to answer for. The magazine invites runners who have entered a spring marathon to apply for a place on their annual Project 26.2. Six successful candidates are provided with tailored training plans, coach and physio support and branded running clothing and shoes. In exchange, the six runners have their training and results followed in several editions of the magazine and are asked to tweet and blog regularly about how it's all going. This seemed like an attractive possibility in the lull after Dartmoor Vale marathon. Lacking direction in life generally and grasping at an opportunity that would give me something to aim for, I quickly canvassed my financial backer (aka my mum), bought myself a place for Edinburgh marathon on 25th May 2014 (fast and flat apparently) and submitted my application for Project 26.2. Surely I had enough interest points to give me a shot at getting a place on the project? Alas not. The competition was stiff and interest factors were obviously present in abundance, so the places went to a cancer survivor, a weight loss champion (5 stone) and a lady who had been training to run her first marathon with her father who had passed away suddenly, amongst others. Oh, whoops, I had committed myself to a third marathon and now I would have to do it without the benefits of being part of Project 26.2.

This would be my toughest marathon yet, both the training for and the running of. Graham and I managed to do long runs together for a while at the beginning of my build-up (although he hadn't signed up for another marathon himself), but then he was taken out of action by a nasty chest infection and I had to go solo. It was a case of needs must; my cheerleading team was on board, plane tickets and hotel rooms had been booked and this marathon needed to be run and ideally run with a PB at the end of it. So I got out there and took on my final five weekend long runs pretty much alone, those being 16, 17, 18.5 and 19 miles, with my final 20 mile run split in half running 10 miles alone followed immediately by another 10 miles with Clare who had signed up to run the Edinburgh half-marathon on the same day as the marathon.

The following are some of the more interesting experiences and memories from my third and, to date, final marathon, my very own Project 26.2.

The Training

Training with the 'talented' runners:

During the last few cycles of marathon training, Nick had mentioned the possibility of doing running sessions at an athletics track. This sounded like something that would make an interesting change to road running but the thought remained just a thought for me and never progressed any further. This time around though my son Sam had recently begun attending regular track sessions with a sprint group from Yate Athletics Club and there happened to be a group of adult runners from Westbury Harriers training at the same time that I could join in with, so I did. And I got Graham and Nick to come along too. The training involved 'efforts' primarily intended to help runners improve their times over 5 and 10k distances, but it seemed a good way to add variety to my running week and with an average of 5 miles covered during the evening it also ticked the box for a mid-week marathon training run. A typical session would involve 3-4 gentle warm-up laps of the 400m track, followed by faster sets of a specific distance (between 600m and 1 mile) with jog recoveries in between, then a few cool-down laps. I was mostly bringing up the rear like a true plodder while the talented runners like Nick pounded round and lapped me (many times) but I was pleasantly surprised to find that I could manage a sub-8 minute mile with Graham urging me on and the organiser, Richard, was always supportive and encouraging. The funniest moment at the track was when Graham was talking to me whilst we ran and unwittingly went smack into one of the hurdles that had been set out around one side of the track. Being made of lightweight aluminium and having been run into from the wrong side so that it didn't just tip, the hurdle crumpled dramatically across the top becoming a zigzag shape. An embarrassed Graham tried some rapid reverse-origami hoping that no one would notice his mishap. How he managed the trip-followed-by-frantic-straighten manoeuvre whilst barely missing a stride I will never know but it was simultaneously impressive and flipping hilarious.

Running a half-marathon earlier in the programme:

This time around my mid-training official half-marathon fell earlier in my marathon-training programme. The previous two times there had been around a month and a half between the half and my marathon, meaning I was already running distances over 13.2 miles on a weekly basis, this time there was closer to three months, meaning that I wasn't quite at that point. Could I come close to my PB from the previous September?

It turned out to be a hard race, feeling a lot more gritty and tough than my flying 1:52 six months before. I couldn't keep pace with Graham and lost him in the crowd of runners on the second lap but I still managed a respectable 1:55.

Hitting the snooze button:

I definitely had to work hard at getting myself through the marathon run-up this time, being without a training partner or a motivational goal. It was tough to get out of bed and run and I confess that there may have been some repeated hitting of the snooze button that went on. The bottom line though was that I knew beyond a doubt that it was faithfully running all my training miles that had got me ready for my previous two marathons and it would serve me well again this time. Harking back to my earlier reflections on scary running, trying to complete a marathon without adequate training would definitely be scary running and that thought alone probably kept me going. Well that and the fact that flight tickets and hotel rooms in Edinburgh had already been booked and paid for.

Running and obsession:

By this point in my marathon series I had fallen deeply into the trap of obsessing over my stats, times and achievements, all beautifully facilitated by my Garmin and Strava. There can be encouragement in measuring our running in these terms as we see improvement and find motivation to work towards goals, but there are also pitfalls. Running, even at my very average level, can end up becoming overly competitive (whether that's purely against ourselves or against others) and before you know it you only feel good about your running if you can see improvement, staying at the same level isn't satisfying. Listen to runners talking together and it often boils down to "What time did you run?" with praise only meted out to those who are on the ascendant. If we come to measure our success as runners only in terms of faster times then disappointment is always looming and we forget that how far we have already come is amazing in itself (we possibly didn't like running for the bus and now we can run miles) and is always worth celebrating. Obsessive running also makes us blinkered, what we want to achieve becomes all important and we are prepared to cast running buddies aside in pursuit of our next goal if they are not in step with us. Which is all by way of noting that I could see myself becoming way too anal about my running and hanging far too much self-esteem on whether I felt I was doing 'well' or not. Things were getting out of balance.

Overtraining:

As well as getting out of balance psychologically, I was also struggling physically during my marathon training this time. I certainly wasn't feeling anywhere near as powerful and strong as I had during my second cycle when I was skipping up the hills like a mountain goat. The running felt like a slog again. I don't know much about overtraining syndrome but it is a recognised condition with symptoms including emotional changes, excessive muscular aches and pains, and reduced performance. I wonder if perhaps that accounted for how I was feeling this time, at least to some degree.

Struggling to find the miles:

Striking out on the longest training runs alone this time presented some unexpected challenges, the most frustrating being finding enough miles to run. Sam was attending 3-hour Saturday morning drama workshops in Bedminster, South Bristol which gave me a convenient window to drop him off and do a long run starting in that part of the city and finishing up back there by the time his workshop was through. But I would set out on a loop that felt like it took me half way round the city and then find myself returning to Bedminster 5 miles or so short of my target. Gah, frustrating! I remember on one occasion having to do multiple laps of the harbourside in Bristol city centre to clock up some more miles and another time resorting to running up and down one particular stretch of pavement until I hit my magical distance for the day. Of course I could have made it easier for myself by mapping out the runs in advance, but as the famous Internet lady would say, "Ain't nobody got time for dat" (now go and search for that clip if you haven't already come across it).

The Edinburgh experience:

Travelling to Scotland in itself was probably worth going through all of the marathon training for. I hadn't been to Scotland before (apart from possibly as a wee tot, but that doesn't count) and I hadn't flown in an aeroplane since having children (and I find airports and flying really exciting). This was my first experience of air travel since the post-9/11 airport security tightening and seeing as we were only travelling with cabin bags I had to research carefully what we were allowed to pack. Meticulous filling of 100ml plastic bottles with various toiletry products and placing them in appropriately see-through pouches ensued. Time was also spent in carefully choosing the aforementioned cabin bags and making sure their dimensions would be easyJet compatible. I confess to being possibly a little over-excited at owning my first suitcase with wheels and a retractable handle. And to the stand-up comedian who likes to rant about annoying wheely bags and their users (and who shall remain nameless but only because I can't remember who it was) I say, you go ahead and lug your luggage around mate but now that I have experienced wheels there will be no going back; aching shoulders are a thing of the past, you however are welcome to them.

Our little travelling band of Clare, my mum, my eldest daughter Keziah, Nick and myself, enjoyed Edinburgh and, certainly for me, the experience of visiting and running in a new place added a lot to the entire marathon experience. We can recommend visiting the Camera Obscura which was the most touristy thing we did apart from visiting the cafe where J K Rowling spent many hours writing the Harry Potter series (Clare's must-do-in-Edinburgh choice). Keziah, mum and I flew up early on the Friday morning (a little too early for my mum's liking - sorry) allowing us a whole day to be tourists once we had arrived and another full day before the marathon on Sunday. Clare flew up on the Friday evening after her day's work and Nick joined us later too, he was gunning for a sub-3 hour marathon time. I had chosen the cheapest Travelodge I could find near Musselburgh for our base. I wasn't spending my own money so I felt obliged to go budget, which turned out to be an interesting experience (I'm not sure if Nick, who booked into the same hotel, has forgiven me yet). (a) It was in the middle of nowhere and even the local taxi drivers hardly knew it existed, and (b) the adjoining Little Chef and Burger King had closed down giving the whole precinct the air of a ghost town; tumble weed would not have felt out of place. Finding somewhere to eat locally was nigh on impossible but eventually, after hiking several miles to a bus stop and finding the edges of civilisation, sustenance was to be found (I'm not sure if Keziah has forgiven me for that one yet). Ho hum, perhaps spending a few more of my mum's pennies on hotel accommodation would have been worthwhile. After a final lengthy fruitless Sunday night post-marathon walk in search of food ending at a pub that had stopped serving for the day, in desperation we rang for a taxi discovering Toun Taxis and the instantly likeable Tommy who took us to a nice reliable Wetherspoons and was then was booked to ferry us to the airport the next day.

The Marathon in Brief.

Getting to the start line on time:

Having been organised enough to get to my geographical race start in plenty of time, I then nearly blew it by chancing a last minute portaloo visit. The queue for the toilet was short enough that a last pre-race wee seemed the sensible thing to do but somehow, having squeezed out my final few drops, I found that I had underestimated how far I still had to walk to get to my designated start pen and so ended up pushing through the crowds of more organised already assembled runners saying "Excuse me, excuse me" whilst simultaneously trying to wrestle myself into my water bottle and gel-holder belt. I just about made it in time. That being said, that wee (and all those that had preceded it during the morning) turned out to be worthwhile as I managed to run my first marathon without a toilet stop.

The first 10 miles:

I had a comfortable first 10 miles trying (and failing) to hold something back for later. I knew what my sensible pace should be but kept glancing at my Garmin and finding that I was running faster. I would then rein myself in a little only to find a short while later that inadvertently I had sped up again. After a while I just decided to go with what felt natural. My first half clocked in at about 2:02, which was satisfying but perhaps not terribly wise all things considered.

Miles 10 - 20:

Miles 10 - 20 I found desolate and a little soul-destroying. I became acutely aware that there was still such a long way to run and, although other runners surrounded me, I felt horribly alone with the grittiness of the marathon challenge. I was scared that I wouldn't find the wherewithal to keep going and going and going some more. Mentally I tried to break the race into chunks as I started to really struggle, thinking, 'I'll get to the turn where the course doubles back around mile 17 then I'll allow myself a little walk' or 'I've got to hold on and dig deep until mile 20 then I'm into the final leg'. In the end I took my first walk break at around 18.5 miles (caught on camera by the marathon photographers, but I see that I certainly wasn't alone in walking at that point). In retrospect it may have been a mistake to think that a walk break would be refreshing because after that my legs were like jelly and my remaining running was all over the place (as in I completely lost my flow).

The final push:

I got through the miles from 18.5 to the 26.45 I registered on my Garmin by taking strategic minute walk breaks in each mile. My legs felt useless, heavy and spent and my pace was progressively slowing down. I tried to keep hold of the time I had in the bank from the first half to finish with a PB, which I did manage but definitely not in style. Those last 8 miles were some of the heaviest and hardest I have ever run and, to be brutally honest, bloody miserable.

The finish:

The marathon finish was in a park in Musselburgh outside Edinburgh (near our ghostly Travelodge) and having rounded the final corner and passed mum and Keziah cheering me on enthusiastically and seeing that the finish gantry was within sight, I managed a sprint to the line and a time of 4:14:59.

Friendly faces on the way around:

My race highlights were: The amazing Sole Sisters, Clare, Mum and Keziah at mile 9 who cheering me on so heartily, spotting Nick at his mile 21 (my 15), seeing mum and Keziah again at the finish and the huge post-race hugs from mum and Keziah which were much needed after such a challenging run.

The course:

The course has some nice features like running beside the waters of the Firth of Forth and does not include any hills to speak of. The marathon takes runners out of Edinburgh, through Musselburgh and beyond to a turning point at around mile 17 where you explore a little bit of off-road country track before hitting the road again and heading back to Musselburgh and the finish. I would describe it as an 'out and back' style course and for me this was mentally tough. With a winding course I find the twists and turns provide diversion because you don't know what lies around the next bend (unless you are on familiar territory) but with this course for miles and miles I could actually see just how far I still had to go and for me the effect was crushing.

Nick:

What is there to say, he Beasted his marathon and ran 2:55. Well done mate.

The medal:

An unusual jagged dagger-shaped medal intended to represent the hills around Edinburgh. Better be careful at airport security.

Post-race:

I had no blisters or chafing and fortunately few physical ill effects from my marathon-effort beyond the expected muscle soreness for a few days, but mentally it was another story. Despite taking a nice chunk off my previous marathon times, I found the race so hard that I felt traumatised by it afterwards. I didn't want to spoil Nick and Clare's respective highs at their achievements that day (Clare ran a new half-marathon PB which she was particularly chuffed with as she felt she had totally 'winged it' and Nick got his sub-3 hour time), so I mostly kept my feelings to myself but I didn't feel that my heart was in our celebrations, I felt mentally and emotionally battered and bruised. I guess I had my first experience of hitting the wall and it was brutal. My pride was dented because it felt like this marathon had whooped my ass whereas the previous two times I had felt like the one in control. Who can say what made the difference this time - preparation, setting out too fast, too much walking around Edinburgh the previous day, expecting more of myself than I was equipped for - whatever accounted for how tough this one was, the effects lingered long after the day itself in the form of something like post-marathon blues. Put it this way, I certainly wouldn't be signing up for another marathon anytime soon, I had had my fill for the time being. After the marathon I spent a lot of time mentally analysing my performance and trying to find a way to translate what felt like a terrible race into something I could feel more positive about. One of the things I did was to look at the Edinburgh performances of other runners of around my ability on Strava. The app gives a graph of pace against time and I could see that with one exception (a real steady Eddy) everyone's stats showed either a progressive slowing down over the distance or a steady 16-20 miles followed by a very mixed finish often involving the telling graph spikes of multiple walk breaks. It seems that my experience was pretty typical.

My fantastic mum:

Tough running aside, this marathon wouldn't have been possible without the support and backing of my amazing mum. She has been my biggest fan since I started running with Clare back in 2010 and The Bank of Mum (the phrase coined by Nick) has made many of my running adventures possible. Thank you mum.

A Postscript – Summer 2016

After My Marathons

It has taken me more than two years to find a peaceful and lengthy enough chunk of time for editing into shape my marathon musings; such is the crazy-busy life of a mum. Well a lot can happen in two years, good, bad, happy and sad, so now I am adding a postscript to bring my running journey up to date. Some bits of this will be humbling to write honestly because I neither have further magnificent feats of my own to document nor an admirably committed maintenance regime that has kept me in the marathon-running form I had worked so hard for, instead more of a gradual descent into running apathy.

After my experience of running a gritty marathon in Edinburgh in spring 2014, I was in no hurry to train for another one any time soon (although I wouldn't go as far as to say never again) and since then I haven't had any new goals other than to keep on running in some form or another. As it turns out, exciting and challenging goals are pretty key to maintaining the habit of regular running for many of us, myself included, so in their absence things have kind of gone down the pan. That confession aside though, there are running ventures and storylines that have happened in that span of two years that are worth sharing if you've read this far and are still with me. So make yourself a cup of tea, plump up the sofa cushions and I'll get started. Perhaps have some tissues to hand if you are of a sensitive disposition though.

To go in roughly chronological order I'll start with my nemesis the dreaded 10k race, of which there has been a smattering throughout the last few years. A few weeks before Edinburgh marathon in spring 2014 I ran my first 10k since the Race for Life with Clare way back in 2010. I had paid my entry for the Bristol 10k in 2012 and 2013 then ended up not running either time due to illness or injury, but this time I had no excuse for backing out. My primary memories of the race are finding it ridiculously hard for someone who was a few weeks off running a marathon and feeling like a failure because I caved in to the pain and stopped to walk a few times in the final mile. It only occurs to me now I am writing this, but maybe that was another sign that I was generally fatigued from my three rounds of marathon training and not recovering well. My time was 53:52, a respectable pace for me but a smidgen slower than that I ran my PB half-marathon at a little over a year before. I definitely wasn't feeling at the top of my running game anymore.

My next 10k was Chippenham a few weeks after Edinburgh marathon. Nick and I travelled over together to run it. Graham really wanted to join us as he had had a great race there the previous year and had loved it but he had to work overtime (sad face emoji). This 10k was pretty low-key and the course was a mix of road running and country tracks with a fairly steep hill near the end. With a trip and fall that left me with grazed hands and a walk break on the hill, I came in in 56:36. There was no Strava-style kudos to be had from Nick and I felt really embarrassed that I had dragged myself over the finish line so long after he'd finished. Obviously it was ridiculous to be comparing myself to a 36-minute 10k runner and finding myself lacking, but that's what happens when your pride exceeds your training and ability.

Both of those 10k races left me feeling like I wasn't performing well at all and the silence from quarters where I might have hoped for a reassuring "Well done" or even a "Good effort" seemed to affirm that self-judgement. To say that I didn't feel I 'performed' well is obviously being pretty harsh on myself and reflects how tied up I'd become in the culture within the more serious sections of the running community of making it all about the stats; If you're not bringing those times down and chasing the next PB the sentiment goes, well you're just not a proper runner, either knuckle down and get serious or call yourself a jogger. I hadn't set target times for either race so I wasn't disappointed in myself so much on that level, it was more that I wanted to feel like I was running with confidence at my fast pace not like I was having to force myself round on uncooperative leaden legs that after all my training still seemed to be protesting loudly at the audacity of me asking them to perform that particular action.

Surely racing the shorter distance of 6.2 miles should be less challenging than a half or full marathon, right? Not so in my experience, I feel I have yet to run one that I feel proud of. Admittedly I have been relying on knowing that I can run the distance then just getting out there and trying to be fast on the day, when actually the key to running a fast 10k is (I'm guessing) taking the distance seriously in its own right, following a 10k specific training plan and adopting a well thought out race strategy. Trying to pluck a fast 10k out of the air when your legs are only used to a steady motoring along type pace turns out to be a big ask, too big for my legs anyway. Probably if I'd kept up with the efforts sessions at the athletics track I would have seen some improvement in my fast running but they tailed off what with losing my confidence after Edinburgh and giving the time slot to parent taxi driving commitments with Sam taking a year out of his track sprint training to do a film acting course and needing a ride across town.

The final 10k of 2014 was a bit less slog and a lot more fun, that being Weston Christmas Cracker in December, a fun festive run with Clare involving lots of fancy dress, a run along the sands of Weston-super-Mare and a mince pie and a garish green T shirt at the end (I can't bring myself to wear it). We went dressed with absolute event-specificity as...guessed it yet? ... A pair of red and gold Christmas crackers. We didn't break any records but we had a laugh (compulsory) and I insisted that Clare did her famous 'blade hands' sprint finish.

In the summer of 2014 I also ran my first couple of 5k parkruns, one on my own (apart from the other few hundred runners there of course) and one a week later with Graham. Actually I lie, the first time I didn't run round on my own because I fell into step with another runner and followed him for the remainder of the run. I did make sure to thank him afterwards because being able to run round in his wake gave me a focus and helped me to go faster than I would have done alone. Then I shaved over a minute off my time running with Graham the following week just because he has the knack of helping me go faster than I would naturally be inclined to. My times were 27:06 and 25:55. 5k races feel as painful as a 10k to me but they are definitely preferable being over a lot sooner. I ran parkrun only once again in mid 2015 in 26:56 and sadly that was to be my parkrunning over for the time being as my nearest one in Little Stoke just a mile from my home had to be closed down following the local council's decision to start charging the organisers for use of the park. That story got worldwide news coverage as parkruns are free on principle to encourage people to take on the challenge and become more active and this one could no longer continue without having to pass on the costs to the participants. The other parkrun in Bristol at Ashton Court is a hilly course and a lot further from home so I haven't found the Saturday morning motivation for it yet.

Another new thing in 2014 aside from 10ks and parkruns was trying out a running 'streak'. Now to the uninitiated a running streak is most likely not the same thing at all as the first imagining that has popped into your head. I'm not suggesting that I got naked and ran somewhere public. What I actually did was read an article in Women's Running magazine about the benefits of running every day, described as a running streak (in the same way we talk about being on a winning streak I guess), and with my regular running routines beginning to slide I thought I'd have a go. Clare and I were revisiting Scotland in the summer to watch some of the Commonwealth Games in Glasgow, so with about a fortnight before we were due to go I streaked. If memory serves me correctly I ran on 11 days out of a possible 12. When running in this way the distances don't have to be long, the article suggested that as little as a mile a day would be worthwhile and I would aim for 2-3 miles. For me one of the main benefits was that it took the decision-making out of the equation, there was no need to calculate what days I would run on because the answer was simple: I would aim to run every day. It can take a surprising amount of mental effort and determination to make and then stick to plans to run when life is busy and in the absence of a set routine, so this streak made a refreshing change to the 'Will I? Won't I? When?' inner dialogue. Morning always wins hands down for timing. In terms of building strength, my streak was a little short to comment but I do remember that on day 7 I felt like I flew around, the running was gloriously effortless. Not so the next day though, humph. I recall there were runners mentioned in the magazine article whose streaks had been going on for years; I like the idea of that kind of habit, maybe one day. In the meantime the new habit being formed was an annual summer stadium athletics holiday with Clare. In 2015 and 2016 we went to the Diamond League Anniversary Games at the Olympic Stadium in London and we have tickets for the World Athletics Championships in 2017.

Time to get those tissues out now. In late 2014 I fell pregnant. I was 43 and it was a big surprise but one that we all quickly became very excited about, even 14 year old Sam who was initially appalled. I decided there was no reason that I couldn't keep on running as I was already fit and in fact I found that the pregnancy gave me the incentive I needed to run more regularly where routines had otherwise become patchy to the point of being threadbare. At around 8 weeks into the pregnancy I noticed that I didn't *feel* so pregnant any more, then at around 10 weeks I started to bleed and an ultrasound showed that the baby had died a few weeks earlier. We were all very sad. I knew that the risk of miscarriage was always there particularly at the start of a pregnancy, but I had not experienced one before myself. Waiting for my turn to be examined at Southmead Hospital I hoped that this would just be a phantom bleed, distressing but not unusual, everything could still be fine, my midwife had not seemed at all concerned on the phone, but when the ultrasonographer told me she was calling someone else into the room for a second opinion and I read the expression on her face I knew that my hope was about to be extinguished.

Death is so immovable. There are actually very few things in this world that we can't make some impact on however small by strength of will, persistence and resourcefulness but death draws a line and says "No. It's over. There is nothing, nothing that can change this. I trump everything you have". Suddenly I understood how awful it must be to want a child and go through miscarriage after miscarriage. Suddenly I realised just how blessed I was to have four healthy children and not to have experienced a loss during pregnancy until now. After the initial shock and disappointment I counted this experience as an opportunity to have a personal insight into something that affects so many women who often suffer silently and who must process their grief privately in a culture that barely acknowledges miscarriage, particularly early in pregnancy, as being a 'real' loss at all. I knew from reading pregnancy guides how developed the tiny baby inside me was already after just a few months and having opted for a natural conclusion to the miscarriage with no surgical or drug intervention my body really showed me in reverse over the course of the next eight weeks how industrious it had been while the baby was alive. I bled on and off all through that time, sometimes barely at all, sometimes big clots and on one occasion on standing up from a chair at home a huge uncontrollable gush that I was extremely grateful hadn't happened in public when I was wearing my swim official whites at a gala. Eventually after some really intense cramps and a very heavy feeling, I delivered the sack containing my tiny baby into the loo at the sports centre. It was far too precious to be simply flushed away so I rescued it and improvised a container from the contents of my magical handbag. All very bizarre with two ladies casually chatting all the while outside my toilet cubicle oblivious to what was going on on the other side of the door. Pete and I bought a miniature rose plant and a colourful hand-painted terracotta pot and we buried the little sack which was about two inches long beneath the rose with something precious from each of the six of us next to it. I make no apologies for being so graphic in my description, this is real life and if you haven't been affected by miscarriage yourself, someone close to you will have been. Sticking to the heavily sanitised publicly acceptable version of miscarriage as something that barely signifies anything more than the sound of that slightly awkward word is a conspiracy of silence that I'm not prepared to be part of. When I began to share my experience with friends, almost all of them had a story of their own.

I became aware that I was miscarrying on the 28th January 2015 and I already had a place for Bath half-marathon in the first weekend of March that I had booked almost a year earlier. I decided that I would go ahead and run it and raise money for The Miscarriage Association. Understandably I hadn't been running much in the weeks following the miscarriage but I reckoned that I still had enough of a fitness base to get round if I took it steady, so I did what training I could fit in in the time I had, hit a really sensible pace on the day and managed 2:06:41. I wouldn't know until a few weeks later after the sports centre toilet incident that the baby was still inside me when I ran the half-marathon, I imagined that it must have slipped away unnoticed, but once I knew it made the effort and the raising of funds and awareness all the more poignant for me. Although my time was way off my previous two half-marathons, I was really proud of myself for running my most sensible and strategic ever race which meant I got round despite being underprepared. My brother Jamie from my Dad's second marriage also ran Bath that day, his third half-marathon, and smashed out a time of 1:45 taking 15 minutes off his previous time. Someone in the family got my share of the 'talent' too.

2015 was otherwise not an auspicious year of running endeavour for me, the lack of a goal meaning I really struggled to find the motivation to run regularly, it was all a very hit and miss affair. Here's a quote from Boff Whalley's book 'Run Wild'. Interestingly Boff isn't a fan of city road running (understatement), particularly big city races, but we do agree on the following:

> 'Races give me impetus to run regularly - you can enjoy running without much training, but it's less easy to enjoy racing on very little background running...Races give me focus, something to aim for, something to look forward to...Races remind me how to stick at something, how to get to the end of a thing without shrugging my shoulders and dropping out...Races are communal, the competitive urge staying close to the camaraderie of a shared experience.'

I'm not sure why I didn't just pick a race to train for, I think the rest of life just took over and I'd lost some of my passion for running which made it easier to let things slide. By 2015 Keziah was swimming anything up to six times a week, generally in the evenings, I was getting Sam to athletics training whenever I could in the gaps and Zoe joined the evening fray with a stint at a gymnastics club. I had long since had to let my Sole Sisters membership lapse as I couldn't get to club nights and it was also proving hard to run with Graham as the mornings were best for me but evenings for him. Running lost its joy and became something else to fit into a life that was already bursting at the seams, another thing on my long list of chores. In addition I had taken my pregnancy as permission to eat everything in sight, a habit that was not shaken once I no longer had the excuse, so I gradually put back on all the weight I had lost with sensible eating and exercise a few years earlier. But hey, I won't finish this book on a gloomy note, there is still one more exciting and inspirational running story to share, it's coming up after the next few paragraphs.

I ran a few more 10k races in 2015, Bristol 10k again in May and Tyntesfield 10k in the summer. Surprisingly, despite my general lack of discipline in training, I managed to run a reasonable time for Bristol 10k, 54:57. Tyntesfield was very hilly and the most cross-country run I've ever done. There was some walking involved because running the hills and weaving in amongst the trees was a bit full-on for this city dwelling road runner (Boff would have loved it though). My time was 1:05. It was worth running for the goody bag afterwards, no medal or T shirt this time but a fabric drawstring bag that does very nicely for my knitting (how middle-aged am I?)

Autumn 2015 bought a new addition to our family and another running partner for me when we gave a home to Chloe the lurcher, a dog from Ireland rescued by a local rehoming charity. She was estimated to be between one and one and a half years old and in generally good health apart from being underweight. Her back-story wasn't known but somehow she had ended up in the pound and been spotted by Bristol DAWGs woman on the ground in Ireland as having good potential for adoption in the UK. Being a sighthound mix (the group which includes greyhounds) Chloe loves to run and is fast, so I figured she would probably enjoy running with me. She does love to run (well with me it's a cool jog for her, barely worthy of raising her heart rate for) but she also loves to stop and sniff so our efforts together haven't been particularly fluid. Chloe brings our pet tally to four along with Rory the corn snake (Sam's) and Ru and Lola the gerbils (Keziah and Zoe's). We have somewhat frustrated Pete's preference for being a pet-free household.

I've saved the best 10k until last. In May 2016 my mum and I ran Bristol 10k together. I like to think I provided a little bit of the inspiration that gave mum the belief that at the age of 73 it wasn't too late in life to take up running for the first time. A group from her church was running to raise funds towards a hall rebuild and mum thought she would join in. I thought it was very brave to jump straight in with a 10k but mum walks a lot rather than using her car to get around so I knew she was already pretty fit. She had about four months to train, so downloaded a few plans until she found something that looked manageable and was diligent in getting out three times a week to train, starting off with gradually extended periods of running interspersed with walk recoveries and before race day having got to the stage of being able to run solidly for a mile without stopping. The race strategy was always to run and walk but on the day mum surprised herself with how much the running:walking ratio swung in favour of the running and even felt at the end that she could have run more - next time mum (smiley face emoji). It is exciting to see how my own achievements in running have inspired others to give it a go too, the ripple effect.

Hmmm, I think there is one more reflection in me before I wrap things up that pulls together several of my experiences over the last few years and it is around pride and acceptance. I've mentioned losing weight and becoming an ambitious runner and at the other end of the spectrum I've owned up to losing self-discipline and good habits. I felt great when I was skinny, fit and fast and the temptation (from within and without) is to be down on myself now that I'm not really any of those things, but this is the thinking that dogs us as women and I'm trying really hard to break out of it. Not only does this mindset that we are encouraged to slavishly adhere to mean that we can only be happy when we're thin (possibly we're only *allowed* to be happy when we're thin) but it also means that if we do ever reach our ideal weight we're likely to become very arrogant and look down our noses at anyone who isn't at theirs. Been there, done that and I am not proud of myself for it. To coin a phrase that a friend's daughter likes to use, I may have been super-slim but I was also 'up myself'. I think, to broaden this issue further, there is a lot of pressure from many directions within our families and our society and towards women and men alike, to excel; simply being ourselves is never quite enough. Be thin, be intelligent, be wealthy, be beautiful, be important, be successful, be gifted, be something worthy of admiration for goodness sake don't just be yourself because that just doesn't cut it. I hate that attitude but, of course, I can be guilty of it too. I hate (not too strong a word and I will use it again) that too many people have looked at my kids since they were teeny tiny and not been interested or engaged by them unless they were 'doing' something exceptional like putting all the shape blocks in the right holes at two weeks old - what is that about? I feel the tug of it too with my kids that are heavily involved in sports, do they have to be Olympians-in-the-making for me to be satisfied with their achievements or can I name and shame the parental ambition in myself and allow them just to enjoy and pursue their sports at whatever level they choose for themselves? The sad thing is that if we are only scanning with our eyes in search of the peaks of excellence there is so much that we miss seeing and appreciating in others and indeed in ourselves completely. Sure I hope to get running-fit again but this time I'll ditch the putting-myself-on-a-pedestal smug, it doesn't do good things for my character and that's the thing God is shaping in me for eternity, the rest will pass away.

So that pretty much brings things up to date. During the summer of 2016, Sam, now 16, attended an athletics camp for a week in Berkshire receiving sprint coaching from world class athletes (a very exciting opportunity) and I travelled up with him and used the time whilst he was training to install myself in a selection of cafés in Windsor and get my writing up together. The rereading of all my previous entries about marathon training put together with the experience recently of struggling on runs with Graham has been a much needed wake-up call and helped me see how much I've let my running fall by the wayside. It would be a shame to let things go completely having achieved the things I have and, on a purely functional note, time and money constraints still make running by far the best and easiest way for me to stay fit. I've thought about all the many reasons I find myself where I am now and decided that the key to reinvigorating my running is establishing routine again and deciding on a new goal. The goal I don't have set yet but the routine I'm working on with success so far at one month in. Life is too busy for a running club and I've lost my human running partner as Graham has just moved to Ukraine to be with his ladylove, so it's just me, my trainers, the road and the miles. I wonder what the next adventure will be?

The Photo Section

A doorstep pose before my first ever 10k in 2010 with Clare (far right), her friend Paula (middle) and my children Zoe and George.

Coming into the finish of my first half-marathon, Bristol 2010. Silly headgear courtesy of the children's cancer charity Clic Sargent.

With my best friend Clare before Bath half-marathon in 2011.
She's to blame for getting me into this running malarkey.

Training for London marathon in the snow with ladies from
Sole Sisters Running Club.

Have gels, will run…

Running London marathon for Mark in 2013 and looking pretty cool about it considering I'm very near the finish.

Crossing the finish line of London marathon…and walk…or hobble.

London marathon 2013 - Mark's marathon. I did it!

With my four lovely kids, from eldest to youngest -
Sam, Keziah, Zoe and George.

I was pretty chuffed with my post-London half-marathon PB at Bristol in 2013, I really surprised myself.

In the afterglow of my fastest ever half-marathon with
Graham (centre) and Nick.

Would we have looked so cheery if we'd known what was in store?
Setting off to run Dartmoor Vale marathon with Graham.

Dartmoor Vale marathon 2013 in the rain.
In the finishing stretch, it was a long mile.

Getting a bit competitive in the mum's race at our annual
home educators' sports day.

With my fast brother Jamie after Bath half-marathon 2015.

Proud moment - me and my mum after Bristol 10k 2016.

Running Bristol 10 k with my mum. So cool, I'd never imagined us doing something like this together.

Appendix 1

Tips for the First Time Marathon Runner from a First Time Marathon Runner

This is by no means an exhaustive guide, rather information that I've collected along the way and that I hope you will find useful too. It was written after my first marathon.

PREPARATION, PREPARATION, PREPARATION

You CAN run a marathon, BUT respect the distance and do the preparation required. You might be able to drag yourself around a half-marathon with a few months of half-hearted training (here speaks the voice of experience), but try to run a marathon that way and it'll most likely defeat you or be a miserable experience. Far, far better to prepare well and be able to enjoy the experience on marathon day knowing that you're as ready as you can be (and here speaks the voice of a positive experience). When you are tempted to cut corners, don't. If you don't think you have the time or motivation for the training required, perhaps a marathon is not for you, or not for now.

RUNNING BOOKS, MAGAZINES AND WEBSITES

There are loads of resources out there to give you all the information you could possibly need as you prepare for and run your first marathon. In my limited experience, it seems that most running magazines (certainly Women's Running I know) publish articles about marathon training in the run up to spring marathon season and offer training plans to follow. I came across special edition marathon 'magbooks' in WHSmith and I imagine they would also be available in other places that offer a wide selection of magazines. Often books, magazines and websites are aimed more at one particular subsection of the running population so don't just look at one and think that is the only way to do things otherwise you may come away feeling either demoralised or (if you're a 'talented' runner) under-challenged. Look at a selection and find something that connects with the level you are running at or your running aspirations.

CHOOSE A TRAINING PLAN WISELY

Do some research either online, through books or running magazines, or ask friends who have run a marathon before and find a marathon training plan that matches your current level of fitness, your lifestyle and your marathon goals. Remember when you are setting those marathon goals that if they are any more ambitious than simply getting round, be realistic. If you have strong feelings about the time you hope to achieve for your marathon, particularly if it is your first, bear in mind that if you fixate too strongly on this aspect there is the potential for the disappointment of not making your time on the day completely detracting from the amazing fact that YOU JUST RAN A FLIPPING MARATHON! That would be a shame.

Have a copy of your training plan somewhere visible so that you can easily see what you need to achieve week-by-week and so that friends and family can appreciate all the hard work you're putting in. If you have young children you can make yourself a sticker chart and let them add a sticker each time you complete a run. Why shouldn't adults have sticker reward charts too? You may also find it helpful to keep a running journal to record how your training is going including information such as your mileage, route, time, pace, splits, niggles or injuries, the type of run done (long run, recovery run, etc.) and anything else useful. You could use a running app such as Strava as an online journal.

Some training plans suggest that you include an element of cross-training (different forms of strength training to supplement your running), to give yourself a break from the impact of running whilst adding to your overall fitness. In my experience this isn't essential and if, like me, you need to keep things simple you can find training plans that don't include cross training such as the one I used from the book 'The Non-Runner's Marathon Trainer'.

ASSESS YOUR FITNESS BASE

Before you start out on your marathon training, make a realistic appraisal of your current level of fitness and decide whether you need to tack some extra weeks onto the plan you've chosen to work on your base fitness. If your plan requires you to run 3, 4 or even 5 times a week and assumes, for example, that you can already run for 30 minutes non-stop and you know that this is a huge jump from your current fitness level, then make sure you allow time to build up to week 1 of marathon training otherwise you may find yourself really struggling from the outset, discouraged and potentially nursing injuries. Your body will adapt wonderfully to the new demands you place on it, but be kind and give yourself a chance to make those adaptations incrementally. I took 3 months to build my fitness up slowly before starting my marathon training plan and, for me, this mostly involved gradually increasing the amount of times I ran each week until I was at the required number of days rather than adding distance. I also worked on my running form to give myself a good foundation for what was to come.

TRAINING SUPPORT

Training for a marathon on your own, unless you truly love hours and hours of solitary running, is a huge undertaking requiring lots of motivation and mental toughness. So if you can, find some support for yourself through a training partner or a running club. If neither are an option, maybe you could enlist someone to ride their bike alongside you for those long runs or to meet you with water and snacks at points along your route. Even if you don't have a fellow runner to train alongside, it's good to find someone to exchange experiences with as you work through your schedule, someone who loves running enough that their enthusiasm won't wane after weeks and weeks of running-related talk and whose eyes won't immediately glaze over as you launch into another commentary about your route, time and pace for that day. It's not something I've explored myself, but I'm sure there are communities of runners online to connect with if you don't have a running friend whose ear you can bend on a regular basis.

FITTING MARATHON TRAINING INTO A BUSY LIFE

Before you start out on your marathon training, give some thought to how you will schedule the running into your week to fit around your other commitments, work, childcare, etc. The saying goes 'where there's a will there's a way' and I have certainly found this to be true, but do plan your running week rather than starting out with vague ideas then getting to the end of the week and realising you haven't fitted in what you needed to. If you can run at the start of your day, even if this means getting up earlier than you'd like to, I would recommend doing so. You'll feel great for the rest of the day (honestly) and can mentally relax knowing that your run is in the bag. Plus dark, cold and possibly wet winter evening runs getting ready for a spring marathon are tough after a long day at work or wrangling kids. If mornings aren't an option, could you run to or from work, around the school run, or in your lunch-hour? Could you substitute journeys you'd usually make in the car or on public transport with a run? Basically, unless your life is wide open with spare time, I'm saying you've got to get innovative. Any sacrifices you make will feel well worth it as you start to feel stronger and see that your marathon fitness is building. That being said, if your running time is being carved out of time you would normally commit to important relationships in your life, give a thought to the people on the other side of that equation. Consider how you can include your loved ones in your marathon journey and so stay close over those 4 - 6 months of training. This is particularly important if you think your marathon may be the first of many. I confess that I'm still working on this area myself though; it can take a while to get the balance right.

GPS RUNNING WATCHES AND PLANNING ROUTES

I love my Garmin running watch. Using a GPS running watch, or installing a similar app on your mobile phone, is the easiest way to track your mileage, run time and pace. Once the information from the watch is downloaded onto the Garmin software on your computer (or onto an online app like Strava) you can also see a full map of your route, split times for each mile (or kilometre if you prefer), altitude gain during your run and all sorts of other useful/useless information depending on how much you like stats. Some watches also come with a heart rate monitor, which keen people find useful to gauge how hard they are working during a run and for hitting the right intensity for particular types of training runs such as a threshold run. Whether you feel you need or can be bothered with this particular level of information is a matter of personal preference. Personally I don't feel the need and can't be bothered with it. It's great though to download a record of the data for events that you have run. I loved seeing the map of the London Marathon route downloaded from my Garmin after the event. Of course it looked just like the map in the race guide with the famous route that straddles the Thames but my watch provided the solid proof that my very own feet had been round it. If you don't have or want a GPS running watch or phone app but do need a way to calculate how far you are running in order to reach a particular mileage on your training plan, or you want to map out new routes for a set distance, there are websites for runners that will help you do this such as mapmyrun.com

Have a variety of routes that you use - I have favourites for particular distances - rather than just doing the same out-and-back route each time and extending the out section, otherwise boredom (and sometimes dislike of a particular section) may make your running feel harder than it needs to be and dampen your motivation. Don't be afraid to include some hills even if you need to walk the last bit for a while, they may be tough at first but will get easier as your fitness improves. Take them on and conquer your fear. Local running clubs can be a great way of discovering new routes in the company of others and you'll be surprised how many times you find yourself saying, "I always wondered where that road went", or, "I had no idea this road/village/row of shops existed". In other words, running can be a fantastic way of getting to know the area where you live better.

RUNNING KIT

You could easily spend a small fortune on running gear if money is no object, but you really don't need to if it is. As I've already mentioned, it is possible to kit yourself out well without breaking the bank. Think discount stores like Sports Direct, buying online (including second-hand from sites like eBay), car boot sales, etc. It is worth buying clothes designed specifically for running in, as they will be more fit for purpose. Technical fabrics help keep you cool when you need to be and warm when you need to be and the styling enables you to concentrate on your running without being distracted by clothing malfunctions and includes well thought out extras like key and iPod pockets and often high-viz features (you might even get go-faster stripes). You don't need to have a wardrobe full of running clothes - although some people like to - as the fabrics will air-dry very quickly so you can wash your sweat out after a run, hang the clothes up and they will be dry for the next day. You will find that you heat up very quickly once you start to run, so do have some seasonal options. I elaborated on my winter training kit in entry number 20. As far as summer kit goes, I wouldn't generally wear shorts in the summer these days (I feel too old to wear them well), but I am loving them for running in this year and also my club vest that has a mesh fabric around the midriff and keeps me wonderfully cool. Lots of airflow against skin feels great on a warm day. On a cooler summer day (which we get a lot of in the UK), knee or three quarter length running tights are good (for the ladies anyway, I'm not so sure about the Capri-length look on a bloke myself), providing a functional combination of insulation and bared flesh. Running sunglasses are light to wear, non-slip and definitely worth having, they can be bought inexpensively, for example look out for them when there is running gear that comes in 2 or 3 times a year at Lidl (it is good quality and cheap as chips). If you're not keen on holding a water bottle as you run, invest in a belt that holds a bottle (again, cheap options are available at Sports Direct, etc.) or even a hydration backpack. Ladies, you need a sports bra unless you have very little up top, otherwise not only will you have the discomfort of too much bounce, but you may distract passing motorists and cause an accident. Good old Marks and Spencer have lots to choose from and it's good to try on before you buy to get the best fit. I think special running socks are worth buying, having tried a few I now prefer to spend a bit more rather than going for the cheapest option which are generally the cotton ones. Initially I balked at the socks obviously made of 100% synthetic fabric, they felt like those horrible nylon bed sheets people used to have in the 1970s and I couldn't see how my feet would be able to breathe in them, however I was given a pair for my birthday a few years ago and I've never looked back; they fit so much better, are really comfortable and are much less likely to cause blisters on race day (a big tick there). My feet can breathe in them after all. Think carefully about the kit you choose to wear on race day, make sure it has been tried and tested on at least one long run. If you are travelling away to race, you might want to take a few options in your suitcase in case race conditions are unexpected on the day (i.e. hotter, colder or wetter).

RUNNING SHOES

Until fairly recently when considering the best shoes to run in you may well have been advised to visit a specialist running shop for a run on their treadmill so that your gait could be observed and analysed and suggestions made as to your most suitable shoe style. You would then have come home with a highly cushioned trainer with support in all the 'right' places to correct your problem areas and assurances that your running would be enhanced by your purchase. You may still be advised in this direction, but change is afoot (nice pun, hey) and thanks to those who have wondered why runners experience injuries so frequently and gone in search of answers, there is now a growing movement towards the less is more wisdom of barefoot running. In terms of shoes this certainly doesn't have to translate to totally barefoot running (unless you are really experimental or hard core), but rather to a more minimalist and lighter trainer with less cushioning (particularly under the heel, as the aim is to have a mid or forefoot strike), more room for your foot to move naturally and a sole that is more flexible in all directions. Where you choose to sit on this continuum is a personal decision, I think I am swaying towards the minimalist side and as I train for my next marathon I will be interested to see the results.

As with running kit in general, you can get running shoes without having to spend scary amounts of money and in fact (referring back to journal entry 29) you may do best to avoid the more expensive shoes even if you can afford them. If you try on a pair you like in a specialist running shop but can't really afford them, you may find that you can go home and buy them cheaper online. My own piece of advice is to consider buying a size bigger than you would go for in normal shoes, as a cramped foot can't work properly. You don't want a snug fit with the fabric of the shoe being too close to your toes to allow space for a full range of movement. How often you should change your running shoes is open for debate but as a rule of thumb (or toe) when you notice an obviously negative change in the performance or feel of your shoes, it probably means it's time for a new pair. Don't change over to a new pair of running shoes too close to race day, I seem to remember reading that it's sensible to have run around 50 miles in new trainers before marathon day so that they are comfortably worn in and your feet have had a chance to get used to any differences in the fit and performance.

HYDRATION AND NUTRITION WHEN RUNNING

When you run, you sweat. When you sweat, you lose water from the body. Even if you never pour with sweat, you will still be sweating, otherwise your body would overheat. The water you lose through sweating and other physiological processes needs to be replenished as you run, particularly on hot days or during longer runs, or you may dehydrate leading to a deterioration in your performance and the possibility that you could end up making yourself very ill or even collapsing. On cooler days and for shorter training runs, you may find that you can manage without taking water with you as you run so long as you are well hydrated beforehand. You can work out if you are well hydrated by doing the pee colour test. Look at your pee in the toilet bowl, the paler the colour the better. If you are getting a very strong yellow, going towards brown colour (and probably with a strong smell), you definitely need to be drinking more fluids. On hot days and for medium to long runs, you should be taking water with you. You don't need gallons; a regular individual sized water bottle of around 500ml will normally suffice. If you need more on those really long 18-22 mile marathon training runs, you may need to think about using a belt with a bottle holder (or multiple holders), a hydration backpack or employing a buddy who can meet you along the way with fresh supplies. Sports drinks are available with added sugars for energy and electrolytes to replace what you are losing through sweating, but it's a good idea to practice with these if you intend using them on important runs as I've heard people say that some disagree with their stomachs and likewise the same applies with energy gels. Check out the ingredients before you buy if like myself you prefer to avoid products containing artificial sweeteners because unfortunately they are often found in sports drinks and gels. If you look through the various options available on the market, it is possible to find some without these additives.

As well as needing to be well hydrated, when you run long distances your body is also busy finding energy sources to fuel all your hard work. Besides helping your body stockpile energy supplies before your medium to long training runs by eating plenty of carbohydrate-rich foods, you also need to plan how you will feed more energy in on the go as conventional thinking says that your onboard supplies will start to run down surprisingly quickly. Runners often favour energy drinks and/or gels, but if you think you can handle chewing whilst you run, there are also energy bars on the market or you could go for the old favourites like jelly babies and bananas.

Without taking on fluid and nutrition during your marathon, you are far more likely to have that experience known as 'hitting the wall' in the last third of the race, so make sure you give attention to this area and do practice on your longer training runs. Running magazines and books give advice on when and how much you need to eat and drink on the way round a marathon and it will help on the big day to have thought out a strategy and committed it to memory, for example plan at which points on the way round you will take energy gels if you decide to use them. If you are going to use a special bit of kit to carry your own supplies on race day (like a bottle or gel-holder belt), make sure you have practiced with it in advance. Some belts can be a beast to get water bottles in and out of on the move because the holder is at your back, so you'll need to practice your technique for doing this.

Most events will have water stations at regular intervals on the way round the course and possibly also supply you with energy drinks and/or gels. Check the race information beforehand so you know what is supplied and therefore anything additional you may need to sort out for yourself. The London Marathon has 2 gel stations on the way round, but I wanted to use 4 during the 26.2 miles, so I bought a belt that could hold 4 gels and took my own with me. I didn't carry my own drinks, relying on what was provided on the course.

INJURY

This section should probably begin and end with a disclaimer about consulting a qualified physician, which I'm obviously not, so I will keep it simple except to say that marathon training does place added strain on the body and unless you manage to hit the ideal combination of good overall health, committed incremental training, rest, good running form, suitable footwear and sound nutrition (and also avoid any accidents along the way), you may experience at best some niggles or at worst an injury or upset that could set your training back or even in some cases bring it to an end. To avoid the worst case scenario, make a realistic assessment of your fitness to train for a marathon at the outset (do consult with health professionals if necessary) and give attention to all the areas mentioned above that will give you the best chance of getting to race day in full health. Practice tuning in to your body as you run, in ChiRunning this is referred to as 'body sensing' (and is why I find that running without music is a good idea), and also in between runs so that you can catch and deal with any niggles before they become anything more. This may just mean holding back on increasing the intensity of your training while you make adjustments and see if something resolves, or it may mean seeking advice or treatment. If you are experiencing pain then don't just hope it will go away, it generally means that something's got to change otherwise your marathon journey may end before you reach the start line. Most events will allow you to defer your place to the following year if you are unable to compete due to injury or illness, but do make sure you check the event specifications for deferment and fill out any paperwork required within the timeframe specified or you may forfeit your place. Our bodies are amazing at adapting and acquiring marathon fitness, but it's really important to respect the undertaking and consider all the areas that will feed-in to success. Do not try to wing it.

WARM-UPS AND STRETCHING

I am not diligent in these areas, so I will be sparing with my comments and suggest you take advice from elsewhere, except to say that when I am being more conscientious I would prepare for a run by opening up my joints with the exercises suggested in ChiRunning (like ankle rolls and knee and hip circles) and always save stretching exercises for AFTER a run, as stretching cold muscles, tendons and ligaments isn't a good idea. Some folk absolutely swear by thorough stretching sessions for injury prevention and post-run recovery.

INCORPORATING RACES INTO YOUR MARATHON TRAINING

Some marathon training schedules suggest incorporating races such as a 10k or half-marathon into your training. As far as I can see, unless you are a race-addict (and there are plenty of them out there), this is primarily to provide a welcome change from trudging round your familiar training routes week-after-week. It can also be a great indicator of how much you've improved in your overall running fitness during your marathon training and give your confidence a boost. I was very gratified to knock over 10 minutes off my previous half-marathon PB 6 weeks before running my marathon. My cautionary advice would be that if racing for you means going all out, don't put yourself at risk of an injury or exhaustion by entering an event too close to marathon day, keep the bigger picture in mind. If you have a regular 5k parkrun near you, this could be a fantastic way of adding some speed work into your training and, again, measuring your progression as a runner during the course of your marathon journey.

FUNDRAISING

Many of us raise money for charities through running and if this is the case for you with your marathon, collecting donations is another feature of the build-up to race day. Unless you are a natural at fundraising and can turn on the charm and see the money roll in, this aspect of your preparation can be an added stress, particularly so if you have pledged to raise a large amount as is the case with many charity entries to big events like the London Marathon. You are likely to be expected to raise £1,500 - £2000 for most charities if you get a place to run London through them. It will help to give yourself plenty of time to think about how you can generate donations, from the simplest method of asking family, friends and colleagues for support, through to imaginative ideas such as auctions, cake-sales, shaking a bucket outside your local supermarket and head-shavings. Most charities will be happy to give you support with fundraising, from creative ideas to promotional materials. The easiest way to process donations and get them directly to your charity is to set up a fundraising page online (i.e. through Just Giving or Virgin

Money Giving), you can then promote your page easily through Facebook and other forms of social media or by emailing the link to all your contacts. Don't be afraid to keep telling people that you're fundraising; it's often the case that if people don't respond first time (speaking for myself anyway) it has been forgotten about but they do still genuinely want to support you and won't mind being reminded. Lastly, don't panic if you're short of your target on race day. People may hold back until you've actually run your marathon, or as Clare kept reassuring me, they may be waiting for payday.

TAPERING YOUR TRAINING

Marathon training plans allow for a 2 or 3-week period prior to race day where the mileage you are running tapers off significantly. This is to give your body a chance to recover from the intense training weeks in order to be in peak form for your marathon. You may well feel anxious entering this taper period and worry that you are going to lose some of that fitness you've spent weeks and months working on. I certainly did. Relax and trust the expertise of those who have more experience than yourself; your fears are just that, fears. My plan tapered off over a 3-week period, I stuck to what it specified and I could not have felt more physically ready at the start.

THE MARATHON WEEKEND

Race information:

Make sure you have read and digested all the information in your race pack or from the race website well before marathon weekend. There are lots of things to be aware of in terms of planning and practicalities and if you neglect this you might find you've overlooked something important and arrive at the big day unprepared.

Travel:

I am of the school of thought that running a marathon is enough of an undertaking in itself without adding too many extra real or potential stress factors around race day. So if your race is any great distance from home you might want to think about things like travelling the day before so that you are close to the race start when the big day dawns and you don't have to worry about setting off really early, getting stuck in traffic jams, the car breaking down or any other potential hitches. In my book it's always a bit of treat to have a night away from home too and I think you deserve a treat for running 26.2 miles. If that's not possible, give yourself plenty of time to get to where the race is being held and ensure that you have thought about things like car parking and race day road closures. If you are running the London Marathon, you will need to register at the marathon expo in advance of race day in order to collect your race number, chip, etc., so unless you arrange for someone to register on your behalf, you will need to be in London the day before anyway. The expo is also open during the week running up to the marathon.

The day before:

If you can, make the day before your marathon a relaxing rest day, aiming to stay off your feet as much as possible and to eat and drink well. If you have travelled away from home, it's probably best not to spend this day sightseeing unless you can do it all from a seated position like from an open-top sightseeing bus. Your goal for the day is to conserve and build your energy stores ready for the exertion of marathon day.

Eat plenty of carbohydrate and drink enough water that you are well hydrated going into race day. Do a pre-race kit check so you don't have to rush around gathering things together in the morning. Essentials to think about are: Whatever clothing and trainers you've chosen to race in, race number and safety pins (with your details filled in on the back), timing chip and fasteners, water to sip before the start, gels/race food and bumbag or belt to carry them in, clothing to keep you warm before the start (and dry if it's a wet day), special kit bag or baggage label if using the official baggage storage, and your GPS running watch (fully charged) if you want to use one or your mobile phone + running app to perform the same function. Take some time to reflect on all the training you've completed to get to this point, believe that you're ready and let excitement kick any nerves into touch. You can do this! Get a good night's sleep - as much anyway as your nerves and anticipation will allow - and don't forget to set your alarm clock.

Marathon morning:

Assuming you've managed to get some sleep with all the anticipation of what lies ahead and weren't up at the crack of dawn anyway, allow yourself plenty of time for everything you need to do before the off. It would be rubbish to have got through all those months of training then not manage to be where you need to be and ready when the starting gun goes.

If you have young children and can manage to arrange childcare so that someone else is looking after them from the moment you open your eyes on marathon day, that will mean you can be fully focussed on what you need to do to get ready. The last thing you need when you are nervous and trying to get in the zone for your marathon is to have to deal with a 2 year old having a tantrum because their Shreddies have gone soggy.

Check and double check before leaving house or hotel that you have all the essentials. Most times you will not be allowed to run without your race number on (it is your official badge of race entry on the day) and without your race chip on your shoe to track your progress round the course you will officially be recorded as a DNS (Did Not Show) even if you have completed your marathon in an amazing time and that would be such a shame.

Have something to eat which will give you a final comfortably digestible dose of carbohydrate (bearing in mind that if you're feeling a bit nervous you might not have as much appetite as usual), and get this down you far enough in advance of the race start that your body has time to get to work on it to release the energy you need.

Drink but not so much that needing the toilet completely takes over because that is a challenge once you are in the race start area having to join long queues for the infamous port-a-loos and even more of a challenge once the race is underway. Ideally you need to have got yourself well hydrated the day before. On the subject of toilets, most races will provide some at intervals round the course but nobody really wants to stop for the loo on the way round unless they absolutely have to, so from the moment you get up in the morning go, go and go again. Nerves will normally make you feel like you have to do this every 5 minutes anyway.

Before you say farewell to your supporters, check that you know where to look out for them on the way round (they may be able to move round and cheer for you at several points round the course), including which side of the road they will be on and also where you will meet up afterwards. Now go and run your marathon!

Race tactics:

I feel like too much of a novice to say a lot about how you should approach the actual running of your marathon on the day, so I will just offer a few points that worked for me:

- Start out with realistic goals so that when you cross the finish line you can celebrate your amazing achievement instead of beating yourself up because you didn't run a super-fast time or you had to walk a bit. If this is your first marathon, then just completing it is a realistic goal and maybe matching the pace that you've run your long training runs at. Anything else is a bonus. If you decide you like marathon running enough to do one again, you can set the bar a little higher next time.

- Pace yourself. Hopefully you have some idea of the pace you typically ran at during your long training runs and can use this as a guide. Start out too much faster than this with the excitement of being underway and the pull of the crowd of runners; you may pay the price later on. If you don't use a running watch, you will have to either become very familiar with how it feels to run at a certain pace so that you recognise when you're running significantly above or below it, notice your time for each mile as you pass the markers around the course, or follow a pacer if your chosen marathon provides them. If you feel that you've gone out too fast and start to struggle, don't panic and think you've blown your whole race. Slow down for a while and take on board some fluid and nutrition and you may find that your energy picks up at least to a level where you can manage to keep moving.

- Take on water and nutrition at regular intervals. Don't wait until you feel thirsty or hungry, by then you've probably left it too late and your performance will suffer.

- Use mental strategies to keep you going when it gets tough and to convince yourself that your marathon undertaking is doable.

This is something very personal. You may want to draw upon your inspiration for running a marathon, think about causes or people you are running for, or find tricks that help you to tick off the miles and distractions to take your mind away from obsessing over your weariness. Practice mental techniques during your long training runs and find things that work for you. Most likely they will be different to what works for the next person. Don't worry if they seem nonsensical (like me mentally running the last eight miles of my marathon first), as long as they help it really doesn't matter.

POST-MARATHON RECOVERY

After your marathon, your body will need some time to recover. The worst effects (like the inability to walk downstairs normally) will hopefully pass within a few days, the remaining stiffness may take a full week to go, then you are still advised to leave another week or two before doing anything more than gentle exercise. As with the pre-marathon taper, trust the advice of those in the know. You will soon be running again and probably better than you were before. If you want to keep up your running and need some motivation, choose yourself a new goal to aim for or think about joining a running club.

Appendix 2

Penny Greenwood (Sole Sisters RC) – My London Marathon

25th April – D Day!

So this is it, the training, injuries, tears, smiles and moods were all about today and like so many others [fellow Sole Sister Maggie and I] made our way to Blackheath common. We were nervous, anxious and a little scared of what lay ahead.

Two days before the race I realised that we were in the blue pen, it may not been anything to anyone else but if you know my history then you know that 'Blue' was dad's nickname (he always used to wear blue suits) and blue was mum's favourite colour – even my talk when we said goodbye to her was entitled "This is not a blue day!" So for me, this was a good omen for what lay ahead...

As we approached the common I looked up to the skies - dark and stormy looking, perhaps a little hostile. "Are you here?" We made our way into the runners' enclosure; our priorities (toilets, stretching, toilets, gel and drink, toilets...) were planned out with military precision, getting even more nervous I asked inside my head again, "Are you here? Today is the day that I really need you".

Out of the blue the heavens opened, rained poured as we hid inside the changing marquee, with 10 mins to go we left the marquee and walked to our pen. The rain began to ease and my stomach started to churn (probably due to the gel!), and we walked slowly towards the start, I looked up at the skies "Please be here!" I felt my chest start to tighten, the tears slow and discreet (behind my glasses) started to fall – "This is for you mum; I'm here for you!"

As we approached the final corner before the start, the grey skies changed to a dull blue and there they were, as clear as day, sat together in front of me, smiling! They looked (to me) as if they were back in their forties, mum's hair was a dark auburn and dad's face was still pronounced with his trademark sideburns - that he believed would never go out of fashion – and I smiled back, a huge lump in my throat and more tears. Maggie, distracted by some fellow runners (who we never thought would last 26 miles!), did not notice, we reached the start gate and started running – here we go!

Due to the sheer volume of runners our miles were slow, congested, a little frustrating but euphoric. We dived between the gaps inching forward, gave the thumbs up to each other as we found a space and notched up the distance as we travelled along with the crowds. Poignant moments appeared from the unexpected; I called [my husband] Ross at 6 miles to tell him that we had just overtaken Richard Branson, and "Awesome!" we both echoed when we crossed Tower Bridge, followed by complete hysteria when we turned the corner at 13 miles to spot fellow Sole Sisters lining the route and screaming our names followed by a little way further with my wonderful family – jumping up and down on a wall – shouting and screaming their wishes. Another tightening of the chest, glasses back on, "Did you see them too?"

Of course, it comes of no surprise to you all, that to lighten our mood, I had a 'Tena' moment and our mission was to search vigorously for some suitable portaloos that did not present an extended wait to our journey – lets just say that at 15 miles I got my much needed relief and the 'lightened' load present a renewed vigour; "Come on Maggs, I shouted, let's step up the pace a bit!"

The miles, to both of us, seem to pass with ease. At 16 miles we agreed that another 10 would be okay and at 19 miles as we turned into Docklands the crowds of people shouting our names was even more awesome than before, relentless even and in return we waved, voiced our thanks and kept smiling – this is amazing! And then I said/ thought "This is how you're helping me, this is what is keeping me going – all these people must know, surely, that you are both behind this…." Ecstatic at the realisation I called Ross again, "Where are you? We want to ensure we see you again" and then I called Ruth [friend and Sole Sisters member] with the same question. This is what kept us going, kept us motivated, kept us snaking between the flailing runners, kept us on track. At 2 hours 50 mins (precisely!) Maggs asked if it was gel time, "No, sorry Maggs another 10 mins – we have to keep to the plan!" I didn't hear her muttered response, ha!

In quick succession we spotted Jill [friend and Sole Sisters member] around 22 miles, then the family again still jumping, screaming and shouting on the wall, and then at 23 miles the line of glorious blue Sole Sisters tops (it's that colour again!) – We felt on top of the world!

The sight of Big Ben seemed to take forever, we both went quiet as simultaneously we hit the wall and with heads down we approached the run up to the Palace. I turned to Maggs and noticed her drifting away from concentration, I looked up to the skies and silently asked for just a little more support, just this once. Glasses back on, I found my focus again and my 'vocal-local' kicked in as I urged Maggs to keep going, "But I can't run any faster Pen!" she voiced, "Oh yes you can!" was my response….

We turned the corner to the Mall and saw the finish line, I can't describe to you how beautiful that sight is! With Maggs close by my side we forced the last few yards from our legs, I kept my head up and eyes firmly fixed to the clouds – the skies as we crossed that finish line were a brilliant blue and the sun was shining, and we smiled – we all smiled!

Finish time 4 hours 19 mins and 35 second...(not deducting our toilet stop!)

Acknowledgements

My special thanks go to:

Clare for setting the challenge that got me running, for being my no. 1 cheerleader and ace race photographer.

My mum for telling me how proud you are of my running achievements, for being my financial backer and for being my no.2 cheerleader (it was a close call, pretty much a tie in fact).

Graham for being a fantastic running partner, always encouraging and supportive. I think you believed I could achieve certain things in my running before I did myself.

Jelena for being so warm and welcoming to Mark's family after his death, it would have been understandable if you had not been so. Also for sharing with me Mark's own running story and supporting me in running his marathon.

If you have been moved by Mark's story or knew him and would like to donate to the children's charity of his choice, Place2Be, you can use this weblink:

http://www.place2be.org.uk

About the Author

Andrea-Louise Glenn

Andrea-Louise Glenn is 45 (eesh, how did that happen?) and lives in Bristol, UK with her husband, four children, a dog, a snake, a gerbil and a hamster (at the last count). Andrea home educates her children but has miraculously also found time for running marathons and writing about running marathons.

Before having children (and having relinquished her childhood ambition to become a ballerina), Andrea worked as a medical laboratory technician then moved into social care eventually training as a social worker. Other points of interest about Andrea: If she had been a boy she would have been named Kevin, she once spent a summer working in an underwear factory and she is a Christian.

Andrea has always enjoyed expressing herself in writing and with her first venture into sharing her writing with an audience hopes to inspire anyone to believe that with commitment and training they could run a marathon. Don't be fooled by the home schooling and marathon running into thinking she is some kind of super-mum, she's really pretty ordinary; sometimes thinking she has it all together but more often teetering on the edge of chaos and remarkably not tipping over and falling in. She is an on and off runner of very average ability currently trying to find and maintain the discipline to train regularly in the midst of the whirlwind of life. She started to run in 2010 and in her fitter phases has run 8 half-marathons, 3 marathons, a handful of 10k races and the odd parkrun. Other things Andrea enjoys are time with friends, singing, reading, watching films and the occasional bit of knitting. She dreams of a quiet life when her kids leave home one day but suspects this may be the stuff of fantasies.

Read my author interview at:

https://www.smashwords.com/interview/ndrglenn

You can contact Andrea at - **ndrglenn@gmail.com**

If you have enjoyed this book, please leave a review at the retailer you made your purchase from.

Printed in Great Britain
by Amazon